NEITHER TYRANTS NOR TOKENS

· · · · ·

A Biblical Vision of Men and Women in the Home and Ministry

BY JEFF S. KENNEDY

Neither Tyrants Nor Tokens: A Biblical Vision of Men and Women in the Home and Ministry
Copyright © 2026 by Jeff S. Kennedy
Published by ChristoTelic Press
5742 South 5th West
Idaho Falls, ID 83404

Printed in the United States of America
First Edition 2026
ISBN: 978-1-972089-01-9

Cover design by ChristoTelic
Interior design and typesetting by ChristoTelic
Scripture quotations are taken from the Christian Standard Bible®, Copyright © 2017 by Holman Bible Publishers. Used by permission. Christian Standard Bible® and CSB® are federally registered trademarks of Holman Bible Publishers.

For information about special discounts for bulk purchases or classroom use, please contact ChristoTelic at the above address.
Rev. 3/19/26

Dedication:
To Christ Community Church

TABLE OF CONTENTS

Preface

This book was born out of pastoral necessity. For years, I've sat across kitchen tables and in coffee shops with people honestly wrestling with hard questions about "gender," leadership, and ministry. I've watched families thrive when biblical patterns were embraced and witnessed the wreckage when they were abandoned, distorted, or denied.

I know that the topic of Biblical male and female roles has become a minefield today. Some of you picked up this book hoping I would confirm what you already believe. Others opened it with skepticism, perhaps wondering if this is just another defense of the old Roman patriarchy dressed in biblical language. Still others may be genuinely seeking clarity. You really want to know what the Bible says on the subject, and you're open-minded to it despite the relentless messaging from our culture seeking to deny a scriptural perspective.

To all of you, I extend a simple invitation: come to the table.

My aim is to help all of us navigate these questions with wisdom, grace, and fidelity to God's Word.

If you find yourself disagreeing with my conclusions, I simply ask that you engage the biblical arguments on their own terms. If you find yourself agreeing, I hope you'll be challenged to live out these convictions with the sacrificial, cross-shaped love of Christ.

Jeff Kennedy

1
Where Two Horizons Meet

I GREW UP IN A HOUSE WHERE MY DAD'S authority was absolute. His word was law and defying him meant inviting harsh words and a heavy hand. As a young man in my early twenties, I entered pastoral ministry assuming my biggest challenge in family discipleship would be confronting controlling or domineering men. What I never saw coming was an even greater problem— men who were missing in action.

Don't get me wrong, I have seen my share of difficult situations in Christian marriages over the years involving both aggression and withdrawal. These can bring hard weather to a home: isolation, sudden outbursts, followed by long seasons of punishing silence. Each time this pattern of absence and fury plays out, the offender drifts farther from his oath to lead, protect, sanctify, and cherish.

But not all quiet is the same. For some, silence is the bellowing ash before an eventual eruption. Some men never raise their voice in threats or tirades, but they never lead either, retreating into screens, sports, hobbies, or beer while their families drift spiritually. More often than I expected, I found myself listening to the wives of disengaged men who had never learned or refused to step up and take responsibility for leading their homes in the things of God.

What I discovered in homes was mirrored in church life. Now let me clarify that I've had the privilege of serving alongside godly, seasoned brothers—men who soldier into the fray, giving, helping, and teaching. Here at Christ Community Church, where I pastor, many men have answered the call to service in the Kingdom of God. And for that I am grateful.

But this season of strong male leadership has been the exception, not the rule. For years as an associate pastor, I trained and deployed workers into every kind of ministry. When it came time to launch a new small group season, staff Sunday school classes, recruit marriage mentors, or send missionaries, the pattern was always the same. Time and again, it was the women who stepped forward with sleeves rolled up, ready to get to work for God's Kingdom.

Of course, not every woman steps forward willingly. Some, raised to leave all the service and ministry to the men, quietly disengaged, feeling unwanted and unnecessary. The result is the same either way: discipleship suffers when men or women withdraw. But the dominant pattern is clear that where men retreat, women absorb a double portion of the work. Conversely, when men rise to lead and love like Jesus, their families are far more likely to engage and follow. The church is strengthened when both answer the call to their God-given vocation.

Reasons for Disengagement

As I reflect on this, I can see several forces converging to produce checked-out, disengaged men:

Cultural Condemnation: When a man is barraged with the message that his masculinity is inherently toxic, that his strength is a liability rather than a gift, he will tend to check out. Over time, he learns to hold back, hesitant to step forward, fearing that any act of courage or initiative will be branded as unwanted aggression. But there is no such thing as *toxic* masculinity.[1] There are only misbehaved men who drag the notion of manhood through the mud. True masculinity is a gift from God to the world. When properly expressed, it looks like Jesus:

the selfless Savior who loves and leads with grace and courage (Eph 5:25).

Fatherlessness: Today, about 20% of fathers in the home are considered "absent dads," and 70% of incarcerated youth come from fatherless homes. These children are about six times more likely to experience poverty, homelessness, depression, and substance abuse.[2] Men were designed to be raised by a father and a tribe of male mentors who apprentice them into godly manhood. Generally speaking, when boys lack male mentors and never learn to stand shoulder to shoulder with fathers, uncles, and brothers, they lack a vital source of resilience. And so, they are more apt to drift and drop out.

Prolonged Adolescence: When men postpone adulthood, failing to pursue marriage and fatherhood, communities lose their patriarchs, churches lose future elders, and the trades and professions that build the world lose craftsmen. The generational epidemic of boys who remain in basement bedrooms, exhausting their God-given ambition and energies into meaningless wins in the gamer-verse, hurts society and the Church.[3]

Work Fatigue: I have sat with men who've told me flatly, "There is no way I'd ever have the time to serve in ministry. I get precious little time off, and I don't have the time or energy." When there is little balance between work and rest, between effort and sabbath, men burn out. There's an old saying, "A tired dog is a good dog." That dog needs to run, or his restless energy will turn into chaos. And boys are like that. A sedentary, purposeless boy can find himself in trouble. But when he finds a God-given purpose, his work, family, and home life can flourish.

But as he ages and begins to pour himself into his vocation, he can succumb to a different temptation of only living for the job, and the joy of work can become a drudgery. Without the rhythms of work and sabbath, he becomes fatigued and miserable. That dissatisfaction can seep into every part of his life, and the family suffers as a result.

Church Consumerism: We're reminded of Paul's warning to Timothy, "For the time will come when people will not tolerate sound doctrine, but according to their own desires, will multiply teachers for themselves because they have an itch to hear what they want to hear" (2 Tim 4:3). Churches built for itching ears raise spectators, not servants. They produce perpetual spiritual infants, not growing Christians. The Church has regrettably succumbed to the temptation to leave young men in biblical infancy by catering to worldly desires instead of calling men and women to die to self as they carry their crosses and follow Jesus. Mature men in Christ must call their brothers from the bleachers onto the field. They must lead them in the long, faithful obedience that marks true discipleship to Jesus.

Over-professionalization: Church ministry does require men who will step into the role of professional pastoral leadership, but that leadership is never meant to replace the ministry of the body. Instead, it exists to equip members for service. When professional leaders become hired hands who do all the work of the ministry in place of the saints, the church quietly trains its people to consume rather than contribute. When boys (and girls, for that matter) grow up conditioned to consume church as a product, they miss the joy of selfless service, bearing little fruit for Christ's Kingdom. The result is that they just never grow into Christlike maturity.

Ministry Imbalance: Female volunteerism has been both welcomed and indispensable. Without the strength, vision, and perseverance of women, many churches would have long since collapsed. Their faithfulness has been one of the great mercies of God to the church. Yet decades of a wider cultural revolt against biblical manhood have left their mark on men, society, and the Kingdom of God.[4]

The result is a two-fold crisis. In their absence, women have carried burdens they were never meant to shoulder alone. And church ministry has naturally adapted to serve those who consistently show up.

This means that over time, worship may emphasize emotional intimacy, and small groups may center on verbal processing of feelings. Ministry will tend to reflect the relational strengths and interests of the primary volunteers and attendees.

Over the years, I've noticed that many men engage God best through physical labor, doctrinal rigor, and practical problem-solving. Women often excel in ministries centered on social interaction, empathy, and emotional intelligence. The church needs balance in this. To be clear, these are general tendencies along a wide spectrum, not fixed male or female territories. Men must learn to process and share, and women benefit from doctrinal rigor and structured reasoning. People exist at every point on this spectrum, and the church is weakened when either end goes missing.

The New Testament (NT) writers didn't try to erase or smooth over the tension between the masculine and feminine sensibilities; they leaned into it. Truth must still be spoken in love, discernment held together with mercy, justice shaped by a shepherd's heart. Healthy ministry does both: it confronts and it nurtures. It challenges those in error with authority and binds up the wounded and brokenhearted. When men pull back for any of the reasons mentioned above, the church leans too heavily in one direction, and life and ministry become unbalanced.

The Purpose of this Book

If the crisis of absent men is to be healed, the church must recover a biblical vision of male and female ministry and leadership. For some, Scripture's teaching on male "headship" is puzzling and hard to receive, especially in an increasingly feminized and emasculated culture. For others, the pain is sharper because biblical "submission" passages have been misused and twisted into a license to control and to harm. Instead, we affirm that old Latin ecclesial dictum: *Abusus non tollit usum*: "misuse doesn't call for disuse but proper use."

Still, many women carry the other invisible ache of the heart: a longing for husbands, fathers, and brothers to take up the mantle of leadership, to step into a holy vocation of loving, teaching, and leading as Jesus did.

This little book converges on that tension: between the biblical mandate for men to step up and unresolved questions about women in ministry. We contend that male leadership in the home and church, when properly exercised, enables the flourishing of women, families, and congregations. We likewise affirm women serving and leading in whatever capacities the Lord has called and gifted them.

Rival Visions

The role of women in ministry has been a deeply contentious issue within the church, with two dominant perspectives driving the debate: one more traditional and the other more modern.

The historic and traditionalist perspective came to be known as "complementarianism." This perspective affirms that men and women are "equal but not identical," holding that they have equivalent value and dignity as God's image, but are also distinct biologically and spiritually by design. Complementarians argue that these differences are timeless, transcultural, and grounded in creation rather than ever-changing cultural norms.

Accordingly, advocates of this view emphasize a straightforward reading of passages that stress male headship in the home and church ministry (Eph 5:22–23; 1 Cor 11:3, 8–9; 1 Tim 2:11–14), and therefore restrict teaching-preaching in the gathered assembly (understood as the authoritative exercise of the elder's office) to qualified men, while actively supporting women's ministry in other biblically appropriate contexts.[5]

The opposing perspective, which eventually became known as "egalitarianism," takes a different approach. Its advocates argue that all biblical restrictions on women's roles in ministry result from the Fall (Gen 3) and are therefore culturally specific and time-bound. Women are thus understood to be restored in Christ both *ontologically* (as to their nature) *and vocationally* (in their function). Accordingly, their full redemptive capacity for ministry includes eligibility for the office of elder, pastor, and teacher within the local church. Advocates of egalitarianism insist that any past limitations are for the past, not the present.

Though egalitarians generally distance their position from secular feminism, it is a fair observation that egalitarianism emerged alongside modern feminist thought rather than from historic church tradition. The view gained momentum as society's push for "gender equality" inevitably influenced church life.

While both perspectives claim scriptural support, it is evident that they cannot both be correct regarding their central points of disagreement. The Bible's command for men to lead and love their wives as Christ loved the church (Eph 5:22–23) is either a timeless principle of leadership or a time-bound archaism. Paul's command for wives to submit to their husbands as unto Christ in all things (Eph 5:24) is either a cultural strategy—and therefore out of touch with the complexities of modern ministry—or an enduring organization of family and ecclesial life. Likewise, either Paul restricted the role of pastoring-teaching (1 Tim 2:11–14) as a temporary concession to a local problem in Ephesus, or he intended it as a universal restriction rooted in creation.

These are two competing claims about the same set of texts.

That said, this disagreement does not mean the two views are entirely at odds. Significant agreement can exist between the two camps, particularly on broader biblical principles that challenge ancient Judaic and Greco-Roman biases against women. Truth, in this case, is not a zero-sum game. There remains some common ground where the two horizons can meet.

Hence, this book has two central aims: First, to encourage and affirm women in service and leadership within the church, stressing the vital importance of the female contribution to furthering the Kingdom of God through ministry. Second, the book aims to provide a biblical rationale for male headship/leadership in the home (Eph 5:22–23; Col 3:18–19) and in the gathered assembly (1 Cor 11:3, 8–9), reserving the role of elder/pastor for qualified men (1 Tim 2:11–14). It is our contention that these two positions are in no way allergic to each other.

The stance of this book is therefore unapologetically complementarian. We affirm that male and female are equally made in God's image, entrusted with the dominion mandate, and commissioned together to make disciples of the nations. Yet within that equal calling, there remains a creational distinction in role and function. And that distinction is most pronounced in the God-given authority and responsibility of men in leadership roles.

As followers of Jesus, we must resist the temptation to live in constant reaction to bad ideas. Some are quick to recoil from biblical male leadership, weary of its counterfeits. Others have moved swiftly to baptize male chauvinism in a kind of overreaction against secular feminist ideology that now dominates modern discourse. Both are knee-jerk responses. In contrast, our call is to respond with a biblically grounded view of the world. We are called to face hard texts that may offend our modern preferences with fearless determination to get it right.

2

NEITHER TYRANTS NOR TOKENS

WHEN EACH OF MY SONS TURNED TEN, I took them on a memorable trip to a place of their choosing. For Hayden, my outdoorsman, it was Bozeman, Montana. One of our stops was the Tinsley Pioneer House at the Museum of the Rockies, where, for an afternoon, you can step back in time to see what life was really like on the frontier.

Just inside, we climbed the creaky staircase, its narrow walls lined with black-and-white photographs of gaunt and ghostly children. At the top, we found modest rooms, each with its own chamber pot tucked in the corner. "These were their bathrooms, Dad!" We enjoyed that detail a little too much, especially when we realized that my wife had just purchased an identical pot from a barn sale as a flower vase for the dinner table. He made sure to tell Mom when he got home, to the laughter and delight of his siblings.

Downstairs, nearly half the square footage of the old house was taken up by a kitchen without electricity, with no modern appliances, only iron tools, utensils, and a massive wood stove. In front of the kitchen was a parlor where children would play the violin, piano, or recite poetry for the family's entertainment in the evenings. At first, it all seemed so quaint, even romantic. As we lingered and looked more closely, we began to see the reality of it. The front-yard garden was small enough that a single bad crop season could end the homesteading dream. And if it wasn't hunger, then illnesses like measles, diphtheria, or scarlet fever could take out half the children in a homestead.

Downstairs, we found more portraits of the whole family. These weren't photos of triumphant visionaries celebrating their inexorable victory over the elements. The pictures were of struggling survivors. Hard lines etched deep into foreheads. Weathered skin stretched tight across sharp cheekbones. Expressionless stares revealing a vision that had demanded everything from them.

What could drive men and women to risk disease, starvation, ambush, and severe isolation in order to venture west? What kind of dream or promise could justify so high a price? The answer, I believe, lies in both instinct and mandate. We're hard-wired to explore and domesticate—to discover and responsibly develop the world for the glory of God.

The pioneers felt that impulse as they pressed westward, but they did not invent it. That instinct is older than America and even older than the exile from Eden. It is both breathed into our nature and bequeathed upon us as a Sovereign commission.

The Image-Bearing Kind

From the beginning, the biblical author designates one species as bearing God's image and likeness (Gen 1:26–27). But what exactly does it mean to bear God's image?

Historically, theologians have held two perspectives on that. The first might be called the attributional camp, in which the image of God is understood as a set of attributes unique to humanity, including rational intelligence, the capacity for communion with God, freedom of the will, creativity, and social order and governance. According to the attributionalists, humanity is characterized by a set of human traits that reflect God's own nature.

Others have insisted that Genesis 1:26–28 cannot simply refer to human qualities, for not all humans share them. Unborn children, for example, lack rationality and conscious communion with God, and yet they are fully human. Angels, on the other hand, clearly possess reason, free will, and spiritual capacity, and yet are never said to bear God's image.

This second perspective is called the "vocational" camp. Vocationalists view image-bearing not as a set of unique *traits*, but as a unique *task*. Human beings are "imagers" of God in that they carry out a divinely given vocation and fulfill a specific role in the world.

When we look closely at Genesis 1–2, that task seems straightforward. God made them "male and female" in His image and likeness (Gen 1:27), and then charged them with three great commands:

1. Be fruitful and multiply, filling the earth with the godlike kind (Gen 1:28).
2. Subdue and rule the world, bringing the creation under God's sovereign order, exercising dominion over every environment and living creature (Gen 1:28).

3. Live freely in obedience to God's precepts—
    exemplified by the libertarian command to
    partake freely from every tree except the one
    He forbade (Gen 2:16–17).

Here, vocationalism seems vindicated. According to Genesis, to bear God's image is to share a *job description* as the deputy rulers over God's good world. Humanity is God's representative species, His living icons set in the garden-temple, crowned with honor and charged with dominion.

On the other hand, this dominion vocation surely entails certain human attributes. How could humans keep a covenant (vocation) without being moral (nature)? How could they order and subdue creation without rational minds or commune with God without spiritual faculties? How could they obey their calling if not endowed with the capacity for choice? Fulfilling the vocation requires attributes that distinguish them from beasts below and angels above.

And so, the truth lies somewhere in between. To bear God's image is to possess both. Our divinely given responsibilities call forth godly attributes, and the task demands the exercise of certain traits.

Equally the Image of God

Several ancient Near Eastern cultures, such as Sumer, Egypt, Babylon, and Persia, had creation stories as part of their mythologies. The Genesis record remains distinct among ancient creation accounts, most notably in how it depicts human beings. Genesis describes both men and women as bearing the image and likeness of God and given the same mandate to rule over creation (Gen 1:26–28; 5:1–2). They are equally tasked with extending the project of Eden into the rest of the barren and untamed world, to fill it, responsibly develop it, sanctify it, and bring it under God's orderly and gracious rule.

Their maleness and femaleness are functions of divine decree and design. Each person is an "imager," and together they embody the fullest expression of that image.

Equally Resourced

God provides both man and woman with all plants for food (Gen 1:29), an easily overlooked detail that is actually crucial. By granting them both direct access to the same sustenance, God reinforces the unity of their purpose and their mutual dependence on His provision.

This shared access to resources contrasts sharply with many neighboring ancient Near Eastern cultural norms, in which provisions and privileges were often distributed through male-dominated bureaucracies. By contrast, Genesis portrays God's provision as a demonstration of His impartial care and the equal status of male and female within His created order.[1]

Equal Partners and Co-laborers

The woman is described by the Hebrew word *ēzer*, meaning "helper" (Gen 2:18–20), the same term often used in the Old Testament (OT) to describe God's sustaining and saving help to Israel (e.g., Exod 18:4; Ps 33:20; 70:5–6). In fact, this term is never used in the OT to convey servitude or subordination. Many have noted that *ēzer*'s various contexts convey the idea of an added strength or assistance.

Considering its wider usage and the Genesis context, the word *ēzer* means "a proper counterpart; one who provides comforting assistance." Male and female contribute differently but equally to their shared calling. Adam's purpose becomes theirs.

And she is created as an indispensable strength to assist him in this global calling.

One Shared Life Together

The woman is formed from the man's *tsela*, a Hebrew term that appears elsewhere in Scripture to describe two halves of architectural structures including the tabernacle, ark of the covenant, and the temple (Exod 25:12, 14; 26:20, 26–27; 36:25, 31–32; 1 Kgs 6:34; Ezek 41:5, 9; Job 18:12; Jer 20:10). It's safe to say that there is not a single context in the OT where the word *tsela* means "rib" with reference to human anatomy. This suggests that "rib" is a mistranslation or, at the very least, a suboptimal translation. Instead, the text likely points to God splitting the man in half and creating Eve from one "side" of him.

At this point, I should note that some modern readers have attempted to portray Adam as initially androgynous or neuter, becoming fully male only after Eve was separated from him. However, the text presents Eve's creation as adding something that was lacking in him. When we read closely, the story resists modern impositions at every turn.

First, Adam is already called *hā-a'dam*, "the man" whom God placed in the garden "to work it and watch over it" (Gen 2:15). Likewise, the term for man used in Genesis is *ish*, identifying him as the male of the species. He is not a blank slate waiting to be assigned a "gender." He is already male as God made him.

Second, Adam's yearning for companionship emerges not from confusion about his supposed sexless identity but from his God-given task. As he names the animals, pairing them male and female in binary fashion (Gen 2:19–20), he discovers an aching absence in himself, "But for the man no helper was found as his complement" (Gen 2:20). While *observing the natural binary order of creation*, Adam's desire for a suitable companion is awakened.

Third, when God forms the woman, Adam recognizes her not as something ambiguous but as the precise answer to his lack, "*This one*, at last, is bone of my bone and flesh of my flesh; *this one* will be called woman (*isha*), for she was taken from man (*ish*)" (Gen 2:23). The woman is drawn from the man's side and now back to his embrace. Their sexes are biological and creational—assigned by God as matters of decree and design, not of personal preference.

Far from teaching primordial androgyny, Genesis stresses sexual distinction and complementarity as woven into creation itself: man from the dust, woman from man, both from God, and together they, and only they, form a biologically whole life (Gen 2:24).

After being split in two, God reunites the halves as "one body," emphasizing the unity of their biological and spiritual life together. We can think of this in terms of the analogy of the interdependent relationship between the brain's two cerebral hemispheres, each with distinct yet vital functions. The left and right hemispheres work together to process information and perform complex tasks. They are two indispensable and inseparable halves of one whole brain.

Likewise, male and female are two halves of one whole marriage. Different, but equally necessary. God gave Adam the woman so that he could fulfill his mandate, and that vocation requires biological and spiritual complementarity.

A Shared Priesthood

Together, they form a unified priesthood, reflecting God's glory to creation and returning creation's praises to Him. This creation account presents a striking portrayal of the unity and equality of man and woman, in stark contrast to the ancient Near Eastern worldview. According to the creation myths of their neighboring nations, human beings were created as slaves to the gods. Only kings were thought to bear the image of the divine.[2]

By contrast, the Genesis narrative uniquely affirms the dignity and shared purpose of every person as a royal priest, a status passed to all their descendants (Gen 9:6). Genesis presents a vision of man and woman that makes room for neither tyrants nor tokens—he is not her overlord, and she is not his trophy. Revelation shows us the ultimate and beautiful fulfillment of this Edenic vision: the church comprised of men and women made a "kingdom of priests" to our God (Rev 1:6; 5:10), blessed in the resurrection to serve in the New Creation as "priests of God and of Christ" forever (Rev 20:6).

Equally Accountable

Both the man and the woman eat the forbidden fruit (Gen 3:6). While Eve's sin was the result of deception, Adam's sin appears to have been deliberate defiance. Paul makes this distinction explicit when he writes that the man "was not deceived" (1 Tim 2:14), implying that Adam was a willing and knowing participant in the rebellion. Thus, while Paul seems to highlight Eve's failure in 1 Timothy 2 due to her susceptibility to deception, elsewhere he places the weight of responsibility squarely on Adam, "Therefore, just as sin came into the world through one man, and death through sin, and so death spread to all people, because all sinned" (Rom 5:12). By singling out Adam as covenant head, Paul underscores that the guilt of humanity's Fall cannot be shifted to Eve alone. God holds both accountable, directly addressing their disobedience and cursing each with labor-related consequences (Gen 3:16–19).

Equally Guilty

Both the man and the woman experience shame as a result of their sin and attempt to hide from God's presence (Gen 3:7–8). Their mutual shame reveals the devastating impact of sin, not just on their relationship with God but also on their relationship with each other. Instead of unity, their mutual guilt leads to alienation, fear, and the shifting of blame.

When God confronts them, He addresses both man and woman directly (Gen 3:9–13, 16–19). Neither needs the other to mediate their access to God, for they each stand individually culpable. This direct divine engagement confirms the equal spiritual dignity and agency of both sexes.

Summary

From the beginning, man and woman stand side by side, stamped with God's image, equally charged with the task of vice-regency. God breathes into them the same life, lays the same mantle across their shoulders, and sends them into His feral world to bring it under His care. She is not an afterthought but an *ēzer*—a strong and godlike helper to assist him in his task. She is a proper and perfect counterpart. Pulled from his very side, she is not *beneath* him or *above* him but *with* him, two halves rejoined into one flesh, one life. Together, they are priests of creation, clothed in glory, arrayed with innocence, the bearers of a glorious burden of responsibility. They represent the Creator to all creatures great and small, and return creation's praise back to Heaven's courts.

And together they fall. She is deceived, and he is defiant—both eating, both hiding, both suddenly stripped of innocence and glory, now naked with shame. Neither escapes the curse: her anguish in childbearing, his sweat and strength spent in the dust. Their harmony collapses into fear and blame, and side by side they set out on the long march into exile, together as one in their sin.

3

THE PRIVILEGE AND THE MANTLE

EARLY IN OUR MARRIAGE, KERRI AND I never gave much thought to dividing household chores and naturally gravitated to our strengths. I handled my own laundry, did most of the heavy yardwork, and oversaw home maintenance. She managed our family schedule, tended the garden, and kept us on time for everything. I paid the bills and balanced the checkbook. She shopped with a frugality that bordered on genius, always finding the best deals, stretching every dollar. Whenever I had to do the grocery shopping, she'd look at my receipts, barely able to conceal her horror. Her competence in that arena far exceeded mine.

As disciplinarians, we also leaned into our natural strengths. She was the better teacher at home, even though teaching was my profession. I was a better mentor/coach along the paths of life, including sports, hobbies, and church life. It's remarkable how little thought we put into any of it. We simply fell into roles that matched our strengths, and where we were both weak, we worked intentionally to support each other.

That kind of instinctive division of labor helps us see what Scripture means when it affirms both equality *and* order in God's design. Adam's "firstness" as the family's "head" doesn't mean he does everything himself or dictates every detail. His calling is neither abdication nor dominance as he carries a unique charge to set direction. He is ultimately accountable for the home, even as he shares the work and draws fully on his partner's strengths. Both partners are made in God's image and entrusted with the cultural mandate, yet Adam is given a particular charge.

This chapter traces that "firstness" through Genesis and examines how Paul later interprets it— not as a coincidence of the Fall but as deliberate design built into the foundations of the world.

First in Creation

We see that the male of the species was created first (Gen 2:7, 18), a point that becomes significant for Paul when he establishes male leadership in the home and church (Eph 5:21–33; 1 Tim 2:13). To understand Paul's deeply Judaic view of "order," we need to understand what disorder meant to the ancient world.

The Jews' ancient Near Eastern neighbors viewed the supernatural realm as the battlefield of the gods, with the gods often vying for the helm of the cosmos.[1] Ancient Mesopotamians believed that the gods' endless struggle for dominance resulted in constant disruption of provincial life through chaotic forces. Events we categorize as natural disasters (floods, volcanic eruptions, and famines, etc.) were understood as the earthly aftermath of divine conflict in the supernatural realm. The world was out of control because the gods fought over it for power and dominance.

Genesis contrasts sharply with this ancient belief. One opens its pages to discover not a roiling chaos with endless cosmic dust-ups, but a singular-creator-God whose Spirit hovers over the perfectly calm seas. All is at rest and calm under Yahweh's rule.

In the Hebrew mindset, God's sovereign rule could be seen in the beauty of an ordered system. The man was formed first, then the woman was formed as his counterpart. This sequence was no mere rhetorical flourish, but a reflection of that divine order. Genesis 2 fills in the picture: Adam at work in the garden, naming the creatures, yet all the while feeling an unnamable void within him.

First in Calling

The act of naming signifies authority as it reflects Adam's divinely appointed position.[2] Unlike today, the act of naming something held deep significance in the ancient world. Moses observes this very pattern as God creates and then names: the "light" is named "Day," the darkness "Night," the expanse "Sky," and the dry ground "Earth." For the ancient Hebrews, this signaled God's exercise of executive authority over nature.

Ancient kings variously renamed their subjects to assign or reassign significance to them within their pagan belief systems. After being taken captive, Daniel and his companions are renamed after the gods of Babylon (Dan 1:7). Yahweh himself renames Abram, Sarai, Jacob, and His people Israel to mark their covenantal transformation (Isa 62:2; 65:15). Women also exercise this naming authority: Eve names her sons, Sarah names Ishmael, Leah and Rachel name the heads of the future twelve tribes, Pharaoh's daughter names Moses, and Ruth names Obed. Lastly, in Revelation, Jesus promises a "new name" to all believers who overcome (Rev 2:17; 3:12)—signifying their identity and destiny as God's children. In Scripture, *the act of naming is an executive function* shared by the image-bearing kind, an extension of the divine order.

Adam's role as a natural leader is emphasized by his responsibility for naming both the animals and Eve (Gen 2:20, 23). Although Eve will later share in this imaging role, Adam's priority in naming underscores God's design for his leadership.

Adam is also depicted as the first to initiate the marriage covenant. The reason, the author says, that a man leaves his parents to bond with his wife is *because the Lord formed the man first* from the dust of the earth and fashioned the woman as his only suitable complement (Gen 2:7, 18). Throughout the account, the "first-ness" of Adam is on display.

First to Receive the Command

You might say that God is all three "branches" of His government. As the executive, He is the

Sovereign ruler over His good world. As the Supreme Law-Giver, He imposes binding moral obligations on us. His commands constitute our moral duties to Him and each other. God is also the world's Supreme Jurist, judging every thought, word, and deed according to the perfect standard of His righteousness.

These three roles can be seen in God's command to Adam, "And the Lord God commanded the man (*hā ādām*), 'You are free to eat from any tree of the garden, but you must not eat from the tree of knowledge of good and evil, for on the day you eat of it, you will surely die'" (Gen 2:16–17). The term "man" can mean "humankind" or specifically refer to the male of the species. In this context, it's clear that it relates to Adam proper because God had not yet made Eve (Gen 2:22) when the command was first given.

Later, when tempted, Eve already appears to know of this prohibition. She recites and paraphrases it back to the serpent. Adam is expected not only to obey this command but ostensibly to pass it on to his wife and family. He is their teacher and their spiritual leader in the home.

This male leadership as teacher in the home is later reflected in the great Jewish confession "the Shema of Israel" given by Moses:

Hear (*shema*), O Israel: The LORD our God, the LORD is one. Love the LORD your God with all your heart, with all your soul, and with all your strength. These words that I command you today are to be on your heart. Repeat them to your children. Talk about them when you sit in your house and when you walk along the road, when you lie down and when you get up. (Deut 6:4–7)

In the Hebrew text, every imperative verb and participle (hear, love, keep, teach, talk, bind, write) is in the masculine singular.[3] The broader OT pattern places the formal responsibility for instruction in the home on fathers (cf. Exod 12:26–27; Deut 11:19; Ps 78:5).

Moses is the first commentator on the Shema. He repeats the call to instruct children in the covenant, addressing men directly and charging fathers to bind God's words on their hearts and impress them on their children (Deut 11:18–19). The command belongs to the whole nation, and both parents share in this sacred task. Yet Moses stresses paternal responsibility, highlighting the expectation that fathers bear the primary duty of catechesis in the home.

First in Accountability

After they sinned, God called Adam to account first (Gen 3:9). This pattern is significant: while God addresses both directly, He first calls upon Adam to give an account for what has transpired in the home.

To reiterate, Eve does not need Adam to mediate her conversation with God. In fact, because she *sinned first*, she is directly *judged first* in the account. Still, the text states, "So the Lord God called out to the *man* and said to *him*, 'Where are *you*?'" (Gen 3:9–10). I assure you, this is not merely God wondering where Adam might be. God knows full well his whereabouts. The question "Where are you?" is a call to give an account. This theme of Adam's accountability is echoed in Paul's writings, where he ultimately places the blame for humanity's sin on Adam's shoulders as the archetype of humanity (Rom 5:12–14ff.; 1 Cor 15:21–22; cf. 1 Tim 2:11–12). Biblically, leadership is both a high honor and a calling. Men will be held answerable for how they have shepherded the family and the home.

Does "Firstness" Even Matter?

Scholar Linda Bellville and other egalitarian interpreters dismiss the notion of Adam's firstness because, they claim, mankind is created *last* in the sequence of creation on the sixth day.[4] If "order" mattered, they insist, then mankind would have been created before all other creatures. But this tendency to sweep Adam's priority into the dustbin of irrelevance doesn't hold up for at least the following reasons:

1. Genesis presents humanity as the apex of creation, the culmination of God's creative work (Gen 1). Genesis 2 establishes a sequence of man and woman that suggests responsibility and role: Adam is first formed, first commissioned, and first held accountable, facts that are indisputable. In the ANE worldview, "firstness" often carried primacy as a marker of order, and Genesis reflects that creational logic.

2. When Paul reflects on these narratives, he does not appeal to humanity's place in the *cosmos* but to the man-woman order within *humankind*. He states, "For Adam was formed first, then Eve" (1 Tim 2:13) and "man did not come from woman, but woman from man; neither was man created for woman, but woman for man" (1 Cor 11:8–9). These appeals to creation order and purpose aren't illustrative or incidental; they are deeply theological. Paul interprets Genesis 2 as a deliberate grounding for order in the church's worship and leadership.

3. The Genesis pattern can therefore be summarized as follows: cosmic order in chapter 1, where humanity is the zenith of creation; male-female order in chapter 2, with Adam first, then Eve; disorder in chapter 3, where God's well-ordered world is corrupted and disarrayed by the Fall.

Summary

Adam is portrayed not as a tyrant grasping power but as a leader among equals. The woman is no less the image of God, a partner in the work, yet Adam is called to go first, teach first, and answer first. His priority is not a crown but a crucible—naming, guarding, teaching, and guiding as covenant head.

When men step forward to offer the sacrifice of God-honoring leadership, families thrive, and God's people are strengthened; when they shrink back or become hypocritical leaders, all creation feels the fracture. Adam's role is not a result of mere cultural forces, nor a consequence of the Fall, but a sacred trust placed on his shoulders from the beginning. He is a leader among leaders, answerable before the Lord of all. This masculine calling is both a privilege and a mantle of responsibility.

4

DOMINATION AND DESIRE

AFTER MY DAD DIED, MY MOM HAD TO become everything my brother and I needed overnight: breadwinner, disciplinarian, coach, and spiritual leader. She'd collapse into her chair after dinner, bills spread across the kitchen table, calculator clicking while we thundered around the house.

I remember catching her sometimes, staring out the kitchen window while washing dishes; her shoulders seemed to carry an invisible weight that was too heavy for one person. She never complained, but I could see that bone-deep tiredness mixed with fierce love, the way she'd straighten her spine each morning and face another day alone, working two jobs.

She wasn't supposed to carry it all by herself. No woman is. But she did. And sometimes our mothers must take on responsibilities they were never meant to shoulder alone. Countless mothers know this exhaustion. They know what it's like to long for someone to share the load, to have another pair of hands, another heart invested.

Corrupt Desires

Adam's natural leadership became corrupted into an authoritarian rule, for God says to Eve, "Your *desire* will be for your husband, and he will *rule* (*māsal*) over you" (Gen 3:16).[1] The Hebrew verb *māsal* commonly denotes ruling or exercising dominion, sometimes neutrally (Gen 1:18; Ps 8:6), but in contexts of judgment it often carries the sense of harsh or oppressive dominance (Judg 8:22–23; Isa 3:4, 12).

Egalitarians typically argue that the male's domineering rule in Genesis 3 is the first appearance of male leadership. As discussed in the previous chapter, this cannot be the case.

Yet, others on the more patriarchal side of the debate contend that this word for *rule* isn't a curse at all. It's simply a statement about the creation's design. This, too, is a misunderstanding. The context of the passage is one of dispensing judgments to all three parties involved.

A third and better live option remains: Genesis 3 describes a profound corruption of something innate. What was once natural to Adam is now distorted, just as Eve's natural childbearing ability was cursed. In the setting of divine judgment, loving headship is twisted into overbearing control. The Fall thus turns leadership from shepherding care into an instinct to dominate.

Not to Abolish but to Fulfill

Jesus himself makes this very distinction between the disciples' leadership and the world's: "The kings of the Gentiles exercise *lordship over* (Greek: *kurieuō*) them, and those in *authority over* (*exousiazō*) them are called benefactors. But *not so with you*. Rather, let the greatest among you become as the youngest, and *the leader as one who serves*" (Luke 22:25–26, emphasis added). This last phrase can literally be translated as "the one leading as the one serving." That is, Jesus does not dissolve the male instinct to lead; He redirects it toward true greatness. All tyrants may be leaders, but not all leaders are tyrants. To follow Him means casting off an iron crown in favor of a servant's towel. It means abandoning every urge to subjugate one's brothers and sisters in a coercive, manipulative, or destructive way. The one who leads must do so with the heart of a servant, stewarding authority for the good of others rather than demanding to be served.

Christ chose twelve men as the pillars of His church and redefined their task. Make no mistake about it, this call to service isn't mere *servitude* to others, but the *service of godly, humble leadership* after the pattern of Christ. Jesus' masculinity was marked by courage, humility, mercy, and unwavering obedience to the Father. Men are summoned to shepherd God's people, not by abdicating, nor by aggression, but by leading as Christ led. Christ does not come to abolish but to fulfill the role of male leadership. He does not discard it, but instead redeems and restores creational headship to its true Edenic design.

But that's the conclusion. Let's go back to the beginning, where it all went wrong.

The Labor of Leadership

Back in Genesis, even in their respective judgments, we see the differences between men and women. Both were cursed with labor, but in ways commensurate with their male and female constitutions. The woman's pain and labor in childbearing are increased, while Adam's work is now damned with hard labor in the field (Gen 3:17–19).

Reflecting on these differences, Paul commands the Thessalonian Christian men to avoid idleness and get to work:

> For you yourselves know how you ought to imitate us, because we were not idle when we were with you, nor did we eat anyone's bread without paying for it, but with **toil** and **labor** (Greek: *mochthos*) we **worked** night and day, that we might not be a burden to any of you. We would give you this command: *If anyone is not willing to work, let him not eat.* For we hear that some among you walk in idleness, not busy at *work*, but busybodies. Now such persons we command and encourage in the Lord Jesus Christ to do their *work* quietly and to earn their own living. (2 Thess 3:6–12, emphasis added)

Interestingly, all the pronouns ("you") and common nouns in this passage are in the masculine gender in Greek. Furthermore, the Greek term *mochthos,* meaning "work," conveys "hard toil and labor," or strenuous effort, often associated with male professions in that era.

One caveat here: We need to dispel a popular myth that females in Jesus' day *only* engaged in childbearing and childrearing, cleaning house, cooking meals, and not much else.

Not in Jesus' world.

Though childrearing was considered a high honor and their primary role, women held a variety of jobs in the first century such as: (1) patrons in the hospitality industry (running an inn or a hotel), (2) managers of kiosks in markets selling produce or goods, (3) production and sales of textiles—clothing and apparel as weavers and tailors, (4) management of the home, (5) physicians including doulas/midwifery, (6) musicians and vocalists during religious celebrations such as Sukkot or Pentecost, (7) benefaction of synagogues and public works, (8) as patrons offering their homes or property for essential functions within the body politic. Paul exhorted young women not yet eligible for enrollment in the widow's stipend to remain industrious as well (Titus 2:4–5).

But the kind of "work"—the earth-moving, rock-quarrying, soldiering labor that Paul refers to in the above 2 Thess 3 passage disproportionately affected men, leading to high male mortality rates. Men were more apt to die of hard labor, war, or indentured servitude. Even in their fallen state, men provided a unique kind of service for society and the family, suited to their male constitutions.[2] In both men and women, the Genesis curse touches them right where they were designed to shine and excel.

The Labor of Childbearing and Childrearing

Eve receives a corresponding curse that affects her in two primary areas of responsibility. First, God declares, "I will intensify your labor pains; you will bear children with painful effort" (Gen 3:16). This curse touches her childbearing and child-rearing abilities—her primary calling and strength.

Anyone who has raised children understands this reality: the joy of family life is combined with sleepless nights, constant mediation between siblings, and the strenuous demands of nurturing young lives. The curse strikes precisely where women excel, transforming their greatest gift into both a blessing and a source of struggle. God declares to Eve, "Your *desire* will be for your husband, yet he will *rule over* you" (Gen 3:16).

At the Junction of our Strength and Need

Egalitarian interpreters frequently downplay or reinterpret the language of "desire" (*tesuqa*) and "rule over" (*masal bô*) in Genesis 3:16. In order to evade the clear implication of this passage, they propose the following interpretive possibilities for "desire" and "rule."

Sexual Intimacy: Some argue that *tesuqa* points merely to romantic or sexual longing. Yet this makes little sense in context. Adam and Eve already enjoyed intimacy and were commanded to "be fruitful and multiply" (Gen 1:28). Sexual desire is part of God's good creation, not a post-Fall curse. To read Genesis 3:16 as the sudden introduction of sexual attraction is to miss the point entirely, as it stigmatizes heteronormative attraction.

Dependency: Others suggest the verse introduces female dependency and vulnerability where none existed before. But this misunderstands *tesuqa* entirely. The Hebrew word consistently means "desire," not "weakness" or "dependency."

Besides, mutual dependence was already built into their home from the outset. When Adam declares his need for "a suitable helper" and Eve becomes the literal embodiment of that help, we see a picture of interdependence, not independence, followed by a fall into a state of neediness. The curse didn't create our need for each other. It corrupted the beautiful mutual dependency that was already there.

Equality: Still others imagine that the woman's "desire" is a tragic longing for a return to impartiality, but again, the text doesn't say she'll desire *equality*, but that her desire will be for her *husband*. Since she already possesses him relationally and physically, the "desire" here must be for something else.

Desire for Control

A more convincing reading arises when we consider the close parallel in the next chapter where God warns Cain: "Sin's desire (*tesuqa*) is for you, but you must rule (*masal bô*) over it" (Gen 4:7). The identical Hebrew construction occurs sixteen verses earlier in Genesis 3:16. To dismiss this connection as irrelevant amounts to little more than special pleading. In both cases, *tesuqa* signals a desire to master or control, and *māsal* describes a rule that resists or suppresses that desire, thereby dominating the other. Genesis 3:16 thus depicts a new, fallen dynamic: the woman grasping after her husband's natural leadership role, and the man responding with a domineering instinct to "master" or "control" her. Far from painting a picture of the ideal or introducing male leadership into the human experience, the author is grieving something that was sadly tarnished.

Adam needs her assistance to carry out his God-given mandate, and she needs him to lead, guard, and sanctify their home. But what do they get? A cursed world where the soil robs him of all his energies and creativity. While he should be ruling the realm with his queen at his side, his strength is exhausted into the dust—pulling weeds, fighting blight, wrestling a cursed world that resists his every effort. She needs a gentle and strong shepherd who responds to her with godlike leadership and love. And he needs a partner who doesn't think that her submission to that God-honoring leadership is a result of the curse.

The curse struck right at the junction of their strength and need, breaking them at the axis of their gifts and vulnerabilities.

This interpretation coheres with the broader narrative arc. In Genesis 2, Adam is first formed, first commissioned, first to receive the law, first to name, and first held accountable, indicating his relational headship. The Fall corrupts that good order into a contest of wills. Eve now resists submission as a rival *tesuqa*; the man distorts headship into harsh *masal*.

Paul later recognizes this distortion when he roots his teaching on men and women, not in the ash heap of Genesis 3, but in the beautiful order of Genesis 2 (1 Tim 2:13–14). Headship is creation design; tyranny is its curse. Godly leadership is man's gift to the world, but his overbearing lordship is the bane of her existence. The curse did not invent hierarchy; it poisoned the harmony of the sexes and spoiled the male instinct to rule well.

The curse thus corrupts both partners' original design. As fallen image-bearers, women often wrestle against the respectful submission that was once intended to be a joy. Men, in turn, waver between heavy-handed control and passivity, either seizing too much or surrendering too easily. Both are distortions of God's natural order for the home. And every generation has felt the ripple effects of that brokenness. Yet grace still calls us back to the garden—to the place where lovers lead with gentleness and helpers assist with their added strength, where dominion is redeemed, and fellowship is crowned with peace.

Summary

Ultimately, the biblical vision of man and woman is one of harmony, not rivalry, equality with complementarity, not a blurring or erasure of creational distinctions. The man is called to lead, not as a tyrant but as a servant of all, his authority measured in sacrifice, protection, guidance, and care. The woman stands beside him as his true counterpart, bringing her own strength to bear, completing what would otherwise remain unfinished.

Biological and spiritual complementarity, in this vision, is a fixed and purposeful gift, stamped into creation as an act of God's wisdom. At its best, complementarity *is a view of human equality*. Together, man and woman mirror the order and beauty of their Maker, and together they are summoned to contribute to the home, the church, and in the world God so loves.

5

UNLESS OUR DAUGHTERS PROPHESY

MRS. KAY WAS SO MAD AT ME, I WAS SURE she'd blow a gasket. As an eight-year-old, I was cutting up in her Sunday school class . . . again.

She'd just finished telling us about Joseph's shock when Mary told him she was with child. Kay paused, her voice softened with the weight of the moment: "What do you think Joseph did when he heard this news, children?"

I could not help myself. "That fool shoulda jumped out da window!" I blurted.

The whole class erupted in laughter. But poor Mrs. Kay had reached her limit.

"Jeffrey Kennedy, that is enough! Get out of my class right now!"

I spent the rest of Sunday school sitting in the hallway, staring at the floor.

Here's the thing, though: despite what a terror I was, Kay and the other faithful women in that little Baptist church left a deep impression on me. I never forgot her lessons, even if I made learning them harder than it had to be.

Now imagine this: what if every woman in your church suddenly vanished next Sunday? Raptured! Sunday school would collapse. Small groups would fold. Half the ministries that keep the lights on would disappear overnight.

Any church serious about male headship should also take a serious approach to women in ministry. You can't have one without the other.

Considering the above insights drawn from the accounts of creation and the Fall, one might expect the OT to affirm male leadership as an expression of godly service, to reflect and at times confront the reality of distorted patterns of authority introduced by sin, and to showcase women faithfully serving in significant ministry roles.

And that is precisely what we observe.

Scripture abounds with examples of women who blossomed under godly leadership and those who also endured the disastrous consequences of sinful men. In all this, we can see that God affirms and equips women to participate meaningfully in His redemptive mission, even in a less-than-ideal world.

Women in the Old Testament

In the OT, women such as Deborah, Huldah, and Miriam held leadership roles as judges and prophets. For example, Deborah leads Israel spiritually and militarily (Judges 4–5), while Huldah serves as a prophet during King Josiah's reign (2 Kings 22:14–20).

Some have argued that these passages and examples are too sparse to suggest a normative pattern. Still, the biblical authors had to speak into a broken world, recording the harsh realities of their time while also pointing to God's redemptive purposes and the surprising ways He raised up women to lead and serve His people. At the very least, these positive examples of women in significant leadership roles highlight women's *capacity* to lead and serve God's people in extraordinary ways.

Jesus' Teaching

Many have observed that women were often the principal figures in Jesus' parables, illustrating commendable attributes such as wisdom (Matt 12:42), hard work (Matt 13:33), diligence (Luke 15:8–10), and the relentless pursuit of justice (Luke 18:1–8). Jesus also upheld their dignity by challenging cultural norms on divorce, which disproportionately affected females (Mark 10:2–12). He condemned the objectification of women by addressing male lust (Matt 5:27–30) and commended a poor widow as the very example of generosity and selflessness (Luke 21:1–4).

Jesus' Attitude

Women played a significant role in Jesus' life. He welcomed Joanna and Susanna as benefactors of His ministry (Luke 8:1–3), commended Mary for her eagerness to learn as a disciple (Luke 10:38–42). This was a relatively novel departure from the norms of His time, as most rabbis refused to teach women.[1] Jesus' friendship with Mary and Martha is highlighted in John's Gospel, particularly in the account of raising their brother Lazarus (John 11:1–44). He also affirmed Mary's act of anointing him for burial and rebuked Judas for his criticism of her generosity (John 12:1–8).

When the male disciples fled the scene of Jesus' arrest and trial, the women who followed Him stayed resolute, witnessing the horrors of the cross

(Luke 23:27–31; Mark 15:40–41). After His resurrection, Christ first appeared to women (Matt 28:1–10; Mark 16:1–8; Luke 24:1–12; John 20:1–18), entrusting Mary Magdalene as the first to announce the good news to the disciples—a surprising act in a society where women's testimonies could be easily dismissed or even disallowed in divorce proceedings. Through His teaching and actions, Jesus affirmed their value, dignity, and essential role in God's mission.

Women in the Early Church

In the NT, we see many ways in which women are actively engaged in building up and encouraging Christ's church.

Domestic Stewardship: The NT consistently upholds the female role as the heart and steward of the household, not as a lesser vocation but as a sacred trust. Paul exhorts "elder" women to train the younger "to love their husbands and children, to be self-controlled, pure, working at home, kind, and submissive" so that "the word of God may not be reviled" (Titus 2:3–5). He urges younger widows "to marry, bear children, and manage their households" (1 Tim 5:14), elevating domestic governance (*oikodespotein*) as a form of spiritual leadership. The faith of Paul's protégé, Timothy, is due to the faithful instruction of his grandmother Lois and mother Eunice (2 Tim 1:5; 3:14–15). Peter, likewise, honors the inner strength of a gentle and modest spirit as "very precious in God's sight" (1 Pet 3:4). Together, these passages portray the home as the woman's God-given sphere of dominion—where instruction, nurture, and order are her ministry; where she images the Spirit's life-giving work, brooding over the often-chaotic waters of home life—bringing order, calm, and peace out of confusion. A home where her steady faith holds everything together, making it a place of refuge.

Patronage: In the Roman world, patrons were prominent individuals who used their resources to support public works or communities.[2] Ancient inscriptions reveal that up to 10% of these patrons were women. The NT presents several women who fulfilled this role in the church:

- Phoebe is described as a benefactor (*euergesai*, "honored patron" Rom 16:2), a term also used for royals and dignitaries in Rome and Greece.

- Mary, the mother of John Mark, opened her home as a gathering place for believers (Acts 12:12).

- Prisca (Priscilla) and Nympha are also noted for hosting and supporting Christian communities (Col 4:15).

Roman law required the patron to protect and provide for those under their care, particularly in voluntary associations, called *koinonia,* such as burial societies, business groups, philosophical societies, or homeowners' associations. In the early church, these patrons often assumed significant leadership roles. While not identical to the role of elder or overseer, their contributions were essential to the Christian mission, and their leadership was highly esteemed in the community. Again, the NT seems to make it clear that prominent women held these positions alongside prominent male benefactors.

Prophecy: Women played significant and impactful roles as prophets in the early church, contributing to the proclamation of the Gospel. In both the Old and New Testaments, prophetic activity among women underscores their vital place in God's redemptive plan.

- In Acts 21:9, we read of Philip's four unmarried daughters, who were recognized for their prophetic gifts. These daughters exemplify the fulfillment of Joel's prophecy, quoted by Peter at Pentecost, where the Spirit of God was said to be poured out on all people, enabling both men and women to prophesy (Joel 2:28-29; Acts 2:17–18). Their role highlights that the gift of prophecy was not limited by biological sex, reflecting the Holy Spirit's inclusive outpouring in the era of the New Covenant. Both men and women are Spirit-gifted children of God.

- Similarly, 1 Corinthians 11:5 acknowledges that women prayed and prophesied in the Corinthian church. Paul's instructions to women engaging in this public ministry suggest their contributions were normal and expected. While the passage also addresses cultural norms, such as head coverings as a sign of being under male authority, the acknowledgment of their prophetic ministry demonstrates the legitimacy and importance of the female contribution to church life.

(a)postleship: The term "apostle" seems to encompass two distinct groups within the early church. The first group consists of the original Twelve and Paul, who were uniquely chosen for authoritative roles in establishing the church and doctrine. The second group includes individuals who played a role in church planting and missionary work, particularly in cross-cultural contexts.

- Paul acknowledges apostles beyond the Twelve, including Barnabas (Acts 14:4, 14), Titus (2 Cor 8:23), and Epaphroditus (Phil 2:25). This broader use of the term "apostles" includes church planters and missionaries.

- Paul refers to a person named Junia[3] as "outstanding among the apostles" (Rom 16:7). Junia is universally recognized as a female name. The language "among" is a construction in the original Greek that always means "from among" or "an individual singled out within a group." The female Junia was an apostle on par with Barnabas, Titus, and Epaphroditus. And Paul singled her out from among this group as an outstanding co-laborer for the gospel.

- Teaching and Instruction: Women were active teachers in the early church, and the NT gives us several examples of them deploying this gift within the body. An example is Priscilla who, alongside her husband Aquila, instructed the learned and well-liked Apollos. She helped to deepen his understanding of the Gospel (Acts 18:24–26).

- Older women in Crete were tasked with teaching younger women (Titus 2:3–5). This instruction is set within the context of all believers being encouraged to mature in their faith so that they can teach one another (Col 3:16; Rom 15:14; Heb 5:12). We also note that prophecy served as a form of teaching, "For you can all prophesy one by one, so that all may learn (*manthanōsin*) and all be encouraged" (1 Cor 14:31). This term for "learn" is *manthano* in Greek and is the NT word for discipleship education.

Deaconesses: Women served as deacons in the church, a role recognized for its leadership and service second only to elders and pastors.

- Phoebe is explicitly identified as a deacon (Rom 16:1).

- We also note that women led public prayer (1 Cor 11:5), served as prayer warriors (1 Tim 5:5), and were renowned for their mercy and hospitality ministry in the church (1 Tim 5:10).

- Deaconesses were also specifically entrusted with teaching younger women (1 Tim 5; Titus 2:3–4), and familial instruction by mothers and grandmothers played a vital role in shaping the faith of younger generations, including Timothy (2 Tim 1:5; 3:14–15).[4]

Thus, the Bible affirms women in various teaching roles while never overstepping certain creational boundaries.

***Coworkers*:** While the term "coworker" is not an official leadership title in the NT, it nevertheless holds deep significance. Paul frequently acknowledges women as his co-laborers in ministry.

- In 1 Thess 5:12, he instructs the church to "respect those who labor among you and lead (*proistamenous*) you in the Lord and admonish you, and to esteem them beyond measure because of their work." Labor and leadership often went hand-in-hand. The word for "lead" here is the same term that appears in other contexts, where Paul instructs them to "let the leaders lead" (Rom 12).

- Several women are commended for their labor in the Gospel: Tryphena, Tryphosa, and Persis are described as those who "work hard in the Lord" (Rom 16:12). This language mirrors Paul's descriptions of male ministers, indicating equal recognition of their ministry efforts. Women and men alike are called coworkers (Rom 16:3, 9, 21; 1 Cor 3:9; Phil 4:3; Col 4:11), described as "hard workers" (1 Cor 4:12; 1 Thess 5:12), and commended for risking their lives for the Gospel (Rom 16:3–4), "contending at [Paul's] side" (Phil 4:3).

Summary

From Eve to Mary Magdalene, from Deborah the judge to Phoebe the Roman deacon, the story of Scripture resounds with women called, saved, and sent. They endure the wounds of the Fall, yet time and again God clothes them with courage, entrusts them with His word, and strategically places them in various places to accomplish His redemptive work. They are prophets, patrons, missionaries, deacons, teachers, co-laborers, and keepers of the faith across generations. They pray, they proclaim, and they give tirelessly. On occasions when men faltered, they stood fast. As Christ hung dying, they did not flee. When the stone rolled away, they were the first to bear witness and the first entrusted with the message of the resurrection.

The testimony of the Bible is unmistakable: the work of God is never carried by men alone. Women are crucial players in the story of redemption and Christ's mission. Their voices, their hands, their faith, and their endurance are all essential to the success of the gospel. Together with their brothers, they carry the message of Christ's saving Lordship into a dying world. The promise of the Father was to enable them for Spirit-filled ministry. Indeed, the

Spirit's outpouring is proven in this very sign—the
world cannot know that Christ has come unless our
daughters also prophesy (Joel 2:28; Acts 2:17).

6

NOT A GOD OF DISORDER

WHEN I WAS AN AVOWED EGALITARIAN, I would argue my case to anyone who'd listen. I churned out research papers in seminary and relished sparring with my traditionalist friends on the matter.

But every path I took kept leading me to the same dead ends. No matter how good a case I made for women in *ministry* (see previous chapter), I always ran into the wall of those passages in the NT that seemed to insist on male headship in the home and in ministry.

Years after I fully converted to my current position, I once remarked to my wife, "Honey, did it ever occur to you that even when we were egalitarian in theory, we always practiced complementarianism in our home life?" She agreed.

We just couldn't shake the natural order of things, as she typically followed my lead as head of the house, and I deferred to her wisdom and gifts in managing the home as its C.O.O.

Alongside Scripture's rich affirmation of women, we also encounter texts that seem to speak with unbending clarity: male leadership is presented as the norm among equals. What Scripture calls "headship" is often associated with the idea of "hierarchy," as both terms suggest an ordering of authority charged with sacred responsibility. The English word "hierarchy" gets a bad rap in the radical feminist age in which we live. But consider the semantic roots of the word itself. It's a compound word deriving from the Greek roots "*hieros,*" meaning "sacred" or "priestly," and "*archē,*" meaning "beginning," or "first in authority." Thus, hierarchy literally means "sacred rule" or "holy order."

Before we unpack the biblical concept of headship or hierarchy in its proper setting, we must first face the so-called "problem" passage of 1 Corinthians 14:33–38 in which Paul appears to prescribe general silence for women in church. To modern ears, the words are jarring or even offensive. But if we are to understand Paul's instructions rightly, we must take into account the cultural and immediate contexts of the command. He wrote:

> Since *God is not a God of disorder* but of peace. As in all the churches of the saints,[1] the women should be silent in the churches, for they are not permitted to speak, but are to submit themselves, as the law also says. If they want to *learn* something, let them ask their own husbands at home, since it is disgraceful for a woman to *speak* in the church. Or did the word of God originate from you, or did it come to you only? If anyone thinks he is a prophet or spiritual, he should recognize that *what I write to you is the Lord's command.* If anyone ignores this, he will be ignored. (1 Cor 14:33–38, emphasis added)

We observe that Paul again grounds this prohibition in creational design. With that framing in mind, let's consider some interpretive keys to this controversial passage.

A General Prescription for Silence

The Corinthians had turned their gatherings into a noisy nursery of spiritual toddlers banging away on their new toys—tongues erupting at random, prophecies colliding midair, revelations and words of knowledge interrupting sacred liturgy (1 Cor 14:30). Into that clamorous environment, Paul prescribes silence and submission as the antidote, because the worship of the living God must sound like its Author, "God is not a God of disorder" (1 Cor 14:33). What these Greek converts needed was some old-fashioned Judaic *shalom*, or peace. When Paul wishes the church "grace and peace" at the beginning of his letters, that's more than a rhetorical pleasantry or a nice sentiment. His wish is for God's holy presence to abide with the Church because wherever God's presence is manifest, His grace and His peace abound.

Before we come to verses 33–38, Paul has already prescribed silence for everyone (male and female) in the raucous and disordered services (1 Cor 14:28). Paul insists that in place of this frenzied and confusing environment, they must have order. Their worship must reflect the God they serve.

Some Women Were Discipled and Some Not

In saying that "women are to remain silent," Paul cannot mean that in every sense, for he has already assumed female engagement in the public worship, "Every woman who prays or prophesies . . ." (1 Cor 11:5, 13). At issue in Chapter 14 is some kind of disruptive chatter, perhaps questions being asked aloud during worship, likely by women who had not yet been properly catechized or discipled. Such behavior would contribute to an already hectic atmosphere.

Paul's use of the Greek verb *laleō,* meaning "to speak," supports this reading, since it typically refers to ordinary, conversational speech, not to formal preaching or structured proclamation (cf. Mark 2:2; Acts 2:4). This informal speech can be harmless, or even careless, in everyday settings, but in worship it becomes disruptive and misguided.

We can infer the problem in Corinth from Paul's solution to it. He prescribes homeschooling for these noisy, out-of-line Corinthian women. Instead of disrupting worship with their speech, they can "learn" at home. Now, the word "learn" here is *manthanō*—the verbal root of the word *mathētēs*—a noun meaning "disciple." Discipleship was a privilege extended to a select few in both Judaism and the Greco-Roman world.

We miss this because in our modern era, most people are literate. By contrast, in Paul's day only about 10% of the population could read and write.[2]

In that world, the proper posture for *every disciple* (male or female) was one of "silence" and "submission" to a recognized teacher, not because the student was being punished, but because that was how education worked. The Stoic philosopher

Epictetus called silence "the goal" of every student in the learning process (Epictetus, *Disc.* 3.23.38). Stoic philosophy prized restraint, brevity, and quiet attention as the pathway to mastery.

When ancient writers spoke of "submission" (*hypotasso*), they described it in positive terms as taking shelter under someone's wing. Dionysius of Halicarnassus, for example, employed the term to describe the privilege of living under capable rulers whose stable governance fostered civic order and enabled the people to flourish (Dion. Hal., *Ant. rom.* 2.26.1–3). Men who had the time and resources could seek an apprenticeship with a recognized master or philosopher. Acceptance was a coveted honor, and everyone understood what came next— the privilege of learning in silence at the master's feet.[3]

For women? That door of opportunity was largely locked. Formal education and apprenticeships were mostly off-limits to them.

Today, we wouldn't bat an eyelash if someone announced they'd landed an impressive internship at a prestigious company. We know their participation will involve voluntary servitude just for the privilege of listing it on a resume. But we bristle at Paul's ancient language because we don't understand his world, one that largely shut women out of learning environments.

Far from silencing women altogether in the above Corinthian passage, Paul was trying to educate them in the gospel, even though the Greco-Roman world refused to extend that privilege to many of them. Remaining quiet is the solution for everyone who speaks out of turn, and he insists that women learn in quiet submission at home so that they will eventually become productive and not disruptive in public gatherings.

Male Leadership Even Among the Educated

The women who were privileged to participate in public prayer and prophecy (1 Cor 11:5) were likely those who had already been discipled, instructed, and spiritually gifted for such ministry. Still, Paul upholds male leadership among those who minister (1 Cor 11:3), affirming a pattern of headship rooted in creation itself (11:8–9). He states:

> A man should not cover his head, because he is the image and glory of God. So too, woman is the glory of man. For man did not come from woman, but woman came from man. Neither was man created for the sake of woman, but woman for the sake of man. (1 Cor 11:7–9)

Egalitarians typically key in on a couple of things in this passage—the idea of "head" as "source." But Paul's "source" language clearly establishes *authority* in this context, not just origin. Other egalitarians argue that since Paul appeals to the outdated first-century cultural practice of "head coverings" in this text, any notion of male "headship" should also be dismissed in our modern age. But this confuses the cultural *symbol* with the enduring *principle* it represents. The covering was the local, top-level cultural code. Headship is the deep and timeless truth that transcends the social signal. Paul proves this by grounding it in creation: man was formed first, and woman was created from man, to be his helper in support of his God-given calling.

As noted above, Paul likewise reinforces male leadership in the home, charging husbands with the responsibility to instruct and disciple their wives (1 Cor 14:35), thereby maintaining order in both the church and the household. This raises an interesting point of application in our modern culture, where women are often *more educated* than the average male, especially in biblical contexts. Is it still appropriate for a man to take the lead in discipling women in the home? What if you're a practicing engineer, but your wife is a Bible scholar? Would it still be your job to offer her a biblical education?

The principle Paul establishes is not that the husband must always be the more skilled exegete or the more formally educated biblical student (though who would quibble if they were). Instead, the charge is one of spiritual responsibility and initiative in leading sacred matters. "Headship" in the context of public worship and private homeschooling means that he bears the God-given responsibility to lead in matters of devotion. He is expected to "go first" in his apprenticeship to Jesus, ensuring that the household is ordered around Christ and His Word.

Even in the Corinthian passage, the goal was to disciple those who lacked it. And so, if in our largely Christianized culture we find women already apprenticed and biblically literate, we are all the better for it. Praise God, we don't have to make up that ground. But the husband's leadership in the home is not abdicated nor discharged in such an event.

Rather, like Aquila beside his learned wife Priscilla, he is still called to walk shoulder-to-shoulder, glad to learn and gladder still to lead so that together they may "expound the way of God more accurately" (Acts 18:26). In such a partnership, the order of creation is not unwound; it is instead strengthened and reinforced.

Paul insists on this not because he means to muzzle half the congregation, nor because he's appealing to some disposable cultural custom. He presses it because worship is intended to mirror the very character of God, who is a God of order not disorder.

7

WOVEN INTO THE WORLD

I SOLD CARS FOR A BRIEF STINT BACK IN the mid 2000's. Within a few months, to my surprise, I was moving enough units that my manager invited me to one of those "big deal" meetings with the owner and all the top brass. I arrived early, flipping through some paperwork, and within a few minutes, they all started filing in—team managers, finance guys, the general manager, and finally Mr. Big Deal himself—the president and owner. Instinctively, everyone knew where to sit, and more importantly, where *not to sit.*

Natural order has a way of declaring itself.

I saw something similar at home when my kids were little. Some evenings I'd pull into the driveway and hear laughter spilling out of the windows. On other nights, it was weeping and gnashing of teeth, the sounds of justice in progress. Now, my wife is steady, strong, and loving, and when she had to be the enforcer, the kids knew she meant business. But I lost count of the times I walked in mid-chaos and everything just . . . settled down. Tears started drying. Screaming turned into sniffling. Shouting turned into darting eyes. None of my grown kids remember any act of discipline in particular—but they knew instinctively that when Daddy comes home, it's time to straighten up. I genuinely never intended to strike fear in their little hearts. But they did have a natural, healthy fear of me.

What's the difference between terror and healthy fear? Terror is what you feel when the pilot of your aircraft announces that both engines have failed and the plane is going down. It's a hopeless fear with no possibility of redemption.

But healthy "fear of the Lord" is an appropriate and holy awe. The same kind of fear you experience when climbing a cliff or kayaking in front of a powerful waterfall. The knowledge that the very thing you're made to enjoy could also, in an instant, claim your life. Your laughter and pleasure are mixed with a sense of holy alarm. There is a trembling kind of awe in realizing that the God who made all things, who fills our souls with joy and calls us His children, is the very One of whom Jesus said, "Do not fear those who can kill the body only. But fear the one who can destroy both body and soul in hell" (Matt 10:28).

No matter how calm or shepherding of a tone I took in the home, there was something about my presence in the room that was undeniable. Today, I have a great relationship with all of them (and they generally think I was a pretty cool dad).

This really isn't about personality types or natural charisma because some of the most effective fathers I know are quiet, gentle men who lead through steady presence rather than a commanding voice. Others are more naturally assertive, and that's okay too. But regardless of temperament, there's something woven into the fabric of creation itself that recognizes and responds to male headship in the home and the church. I really don't believe this is about asserting power or dominance. That's a false narrative in our world, and it is unfortunately reinforced by those who've abused that privilege.

Paul is writing about the need for natural, God-ordained male leadership. And this is precisely the foundation he appeals to when he reaches back beyond culture, beyond personal preferences, beyond even the specific crisis in the Ephesian church, to the very *ordo creationis*—the patterned design in creation itself.

Who Cares Who's First?

Unlike our Catholic friends, we Protestants derive doctrine and practice from three sources regarding Scripture: what it *commands*, what it *commends*, and what it *compels* by consequence. For whatever the Bible directly teaches, whatever examples it gives for us to follow, and whatever doctrines it leads us to by consequence (e.g., Sola Scriptura or the Trinity), we ought to believe. In the case of female elders, we have no direct commands or instructions on equipping women for the role of elder/pastor. We also find no examples of female elders/pastors that would commend the practice to us. Furthermore, we do have one text that appears to limit this role of eldering authority in the local church to qualified men (1 Tim 2:11–15).

Non-Christian critics regularly cite this very passage as evidence that Paul was a chauvinist and that Christianity endorsed a destructive patriarchy along with chattel slavery. A closer look at the text reveals that nothing could be further from the truth. To fully appreciate Paul's claims in 1 Timothy 2, we should consider three things at the heart of Paul's instructions: (1) the contextual crisis, (2) the cultural codes atop timeless principles, and (3) Paul's Judaic creational theology.

The Contextual Crisis

The general context of 1 and 2 Timothy involves Paul addressing the spread of heretical teachings by Gnostic-like teachers who affirmed a strange asceticism in the Ephesian church. These Greek teachers were obsessed with and misapplying the Mosaic law (1 Tim 1:6–11). The crisis in Ephesus specifically involved false teachers targeting "weak-willed women" who lacked proper training in the Gospel (1 Tim 5:15; 2 Tim 3:6–9). The Greek term used is *gunaikaria*, a diminutive form of *gynē*, meaning "woman," and it carries a negative connotation, often translated as "weak women" or "gullible women." Somehow, the uneducated and largely gullible female population in Ephesus had been captured by these false teachers who preyed upon them in their weakness. This crisis had evidently grown so severe that Paul felt compelled to station Timothy there and provide written instructions to bring the situation under control.

Cultural Codes and Timeless Principles

Our egalitarian friends are right to point out that 1 Timothy 2 contains several culturally loaded ideas. Several "codes" must be addressed before examining Paul's prohibition on women exercising teaching authority as elders. Complementarians typically stress that each of the social codes mentioned in this chapter points beyond itself to a deeper and enduring principle.

Lifting Holy Hands: Men are instructed to "lift holy hands," a common Jewish practice symbolizing righteous prayer, taking an oath, or receiving a blessing with fear and reverence (e.g., Gen 14:22; Ps 24:4; Sir 50:20–21). The underlying principle here is to avoid quarrels and to worship with "clean hands" and a clear conscience.[1]

This passage is rarely applied in public worship and prayer today, except for charismatics and a few adventurous Baptists. Yet, the command still has a timeless referent—men are to publicly revere God in prayer and worship. Today, we can do this by kneeling rather than standing, or by bowing our heads in reverence (a modern posture) rather than lifting our eyes heavenward (an ancient posture). Whatever posture is taken, they signal the same inner attitude of the heart—reverence, awe, and thanksgiving. Regardless of the physical posture, the underlying principle remains relevant today.

Modest Apparel: Women are instructed to dress modestly, avoiding displays of wealth or sensuality (1 Tim 2:9). The specific cultural markers Paul references—such as braided hair, jewelry, and expensive clothing—were ostentatious signs of elitist wealth. Even Greek satirists chided women for such public vanity (Juvenal, *Sat.* 6.502–504). In some cases, this sort of fashion was associated with courtesans who used their appearance to attract male patrons (Tert., *Cult. fem.* 2.9). Such displays would have been rare but provocative in their societal context.

To apply this principle today, it is essential to understand the social symbols of Paul's time and their modern equivalents, as jewelry, braided hair, and expensive clothing no longer necessarily carry the same connotations they did in the first century. However, *the enduring principle* is a call to dress in a way that reflects *decency, modesty, and appropriateness for worship*, rather than in ways that draw undue attention to the individual.

In both examples, we see the top-layer cultural codes (raising hands and braided hair with jewelry) signify transcultural and timeless referents— reverence in worship with a clear conscience and modesty in dress so as not to draw attention away from the worship of God.

A Cultural Code or a Timeless Command?

After addressing these issues, Paul reiterates a longstanding policy that limits female participation in one ministry within the church—eldering authority. The context supports this prohibition.

> Let a woman learn quietly with all submissiveness. I do not permit a woman to *teach* or to exercise *authority* over a man; rather, she is to remain quiet. For Adam was formed first, then Eve; and Adam was not deceived, but the woman was deceived and became a transgressor. (1 Tim 2:11–15, emphasis added)

Egalitarians stress the crisis Paul and Timothy faced in Ephesus and the cultural codes Paul invoked beforehand. They insist that Paul's instruction here, barring women from the position of teaching authority, is necessarily time-bound. But their claim carries an important implication—if the prohibition is grounded in specific circumstances, then it logically remains binding wherever those same circumstances obtain, even in the present day. In other words, the restriction would still apply in any setting where similar social dynamics were present (female illiteracy, rampant false teaching, etc.). At the very least, Paul's instruction cannot be dismissed as a mere relic of Ephesian culture.

Learning in Submission is a Privilege

As noted in the previous chapter, formal learning was typically a privilege reserved for men, so Paul's admonition that they "learn quietly with all submissiveness" applies similarly as it had in Corinth. Submission (Gk. *hypotagē*) refers to adopting a posture of respect and deference to the teacher's authority, a stance required of all disciples including male apprentices (1 Tim 2:2; 2 Cor 9:13). Submission (*hypotassō*) is also prescribed universally in the church (Eph 5:21; 1 Pet 5:5), and Christ himself is voluntarily submitted to the Father in the incarnation as "the head of Christ is God" (1 Cor 11:3; 15:28; see also John 6:38; Phil 2:5–8). Disciples of recognized philosophers were expected to submit to their master's teaching and way of life, and this was considered a privilege for those seeking education.

Far from an endorsement of male authoritarianism, this posture of surrender reflects humility and teachability. And Paul says that Christian women were now honored to engage in this practice through full submission and quiet learning, just as the men had done before them. Until this education in the gospel was complete, it would be (universally) inappropriate for them to presume to teach younger women (1 Tim 5:13–14) or the church in any setting. Ill-equipped and unqualified people shouldn't hastily presume to teach the church regardless of their sex (James 3:1).

Teaching-Authority

Paul's insistence "I do not allow a woman to teach (*didaskalein*) or to have authority (*authentein*) over a man" (1 Tim 2:12) has been interpreted essentially in two ways within complementarian camps.

First, some interpreters take a *maximalist* view of the text. On this view, Paul was talking about two separate and *general* things that apply in every context of local church life. For them, Paul's prohibition here should extend well beyond Paul's immediate context or concerns (the equipping of male elders in order to edify and safeguard the church). The conclusion is that women should not hold any positions of authority, nor should they teach in any capacity when men are present.

Others point out that Paul often uses a writing style called *hendiadys*, in which two words describe a single idea. For example, when he refers to "my speech and my message" (1 Cor 2:4), he is clearly describing one thing (the preaching of the gospel) with two words. Or when he calls himself "a herald and an apostle" (1 Tim 2:7), he really means "an apostolic herald." In the same way, "teaching" and "authority" (2:12) should be viewed as a hendiadys—the *authoritative teaching role* of an elder in the church. Thus, the preferable view is that "teaching" and "authority" describe one thing here, and we should not extend Paul's command beyond

Paul's context. Should we do so, we will need to introduce a limiting principle that is not present in this text. The problem is that this approach is eisegetical (reading meaning into) rather than exegetical (reading meaning out of it). As stated, it cannot be maintained. There are various ways in which women lead with authority and teach when boys and men are present. The main thrust of *this text* is to limit the exercise of elder authority in the local church to men who are qualified to lead and teach the church *in that capacity*.

Four Notable Egalitarian Missteps

Those who view Paul's instructions in 1 Timothy 2:11–14 as a temporary, culture-bound restriction often make several interpretive missteps here.

1. They must read the prior cultural codes of lifting holy hands (v. 8) and female dress (v.9) as *merely top-level social customs*, with *no underlying transcultural principles*. As noted, this cannot be the case. The timeless principles of reverential prayer and avoiding self-promotion in worship remain unchanged, regardless of the social norms prevailing at that time.
2. Egalitarians also place too much weight on the word *authentein* ("to have authority"), insisting

that it must be a decisively negative term. Yet Paul had stronger words available if he wanted to stress domineering behavior, terms like *katadynasteuō* ("to exploit or tyrannize," Acts 10:38; James 2:6) or *katakurieuō* ("to lord over," Matt 20:25; 1 Pet 5:3). Even if *authentein* does skew negatively, it would seem that the complementarian point still stands. Paul warns against any teaching that inappropriately seizes authority not rightfully given. For any female to presume to pastor a church is an exercise in *authentein*—that is, to assume a position of governing authority and doctrinal oversight that Scripture reserves for qualified men, thereby stepping outside the order God established for the household of faith. In that sense, a word with a slightly sharper edge fits his purpose well.

3. Egalitarians must separate 1 Timothy 2:11–14 from its immediate context in the gathered worship of the church (chapter 2) and the qualifications for elders and deacons (chapter 3). Yet Paul's sequence is deliberate: immediately after addressing the issue of "teaching and authority" between men and women, he outlines the qualifications for overseers (qualified men, 3:1–7) and then for deacons (both male and female, 3:8–12, with v.

11). This progression shows that Paul's restriction in 2:11–14 pertains directly to the public worship setting (2:1–10) and the office of elder (3:1–7). In that light, "teaching and authority" should be read as a single concept—"teaching with elder authority." Paul is not prohibiting all teaching by women but limiting the exercise of authoritative, governing instruction reserved for the elders when the church gathers.

4. Egalitarians must detach Paul's reasoning from the creation account in Genesis 1–2, reducing Adam and Eve to a mere rhetorical illustration rather than a theological foundation.[2] Yet Paul, as a Torah-trained Jew shaped by a Genesis 1–3 worldview, does not employ the creation story as an analogy of convenience. He grounds his instruction in a robust Judeo-Christian theology of creational design.

This final point deserves closer attention, for the egalitarian view hinges on treating Paul's restriction as a polemical response to a passing, temporary crisis. If that's the case, certain implications must be faced.

First, it raises the question of how an apostle, under the inspiration of the Holy Spirit, could endorse an arrangement (male headship) that is rooted in a sinful human enterprise rather than in creation. If male leadership is merely the result of the Fall, always viewed as male "domination," then it cannot be commended, even temporarily, without implicating Paul in real moral compromise. To argue that Paul intended this merely as a concession to finite cultural pressures does not absolve him of apparently prescribing something that was (on the egalitarian view), evil and degrading to women.[3]

Secondly, adopting the view that Paul merely used Adam and Eve as analogies in a rhetorical strategy suggests that Paul had become so de-Judaized (detached from his Jewish roots and upbringing) that he no longer saw Scripture as the authoritative foundation for doctrine, but merely as a collection of useful fictions. On this reading, Paul wasn't Christianity's foremost theologian. He was just one of many skilled orators, grasping for a convenient metaphor to get his point across. Such a reductionist view falls short of the rich, complex portrayal of Paul in the NT as Christianity's foremost biblical theologian.

But Paul wrote, not as an orator in search of a handy illustration, but a theologian whose view of human relationships had been profoundly shaped by his Jewish covenant and creational stories.

Thirdly, the egalitarian position faces a glaring inconsistency. If the NT authors were cultural revolutionaries who fearlessly challenged oppressive "gender norms" in the area of ministry and spiritual gifts (which isn't controversial), why is there complete silence about advocating for female elders here? The egalitarian explanation requires us to believe that these same bold apostles, who had already proven their willingness to confront entrenched patriarchal systems, suddenly lost their nerve on this one issue, becoming cultural accommodationists who compromised God's supposed design for the sake of temporary expediency (more on that later).

Lastly, the egalitarian view asks us to take a passage that plainly limits elder authority to men and grounds it in creation and somehow conclude the opposite.

However, if Paul's reference to the original couple is theological, not analogical, and points to a broader principle rooted in creation, the complementarian interpretation is to be preferred. Genesis 2 not only presents chronological order but also suggests a pattern of male initiative and responsibility prior to the Fall.

This is further confirmed by the absence of commands to equip female elders and the lack of any historical examples that commend the practice, all while Paul gives specific instructions on equipping both male and female deacons (1 Tim

3:8–13; Titus 1:5–9). Far from relying on a single prooftext, this view is grounded in the enduring framework of creational theology.

Summary

This chapter reminds us that God's design is not arbitrary and not a relic of a broken age. It rises from His own character and from the order He set at the beginning. The Creator God has woven order into creation, the church's worship, and the home. To resist that order is to resist His peace. To receive it is to reflect His wisdom. Paul's appeal to creation is not a retreat into male abuse structures but a return to harmony before the Fall, where male "headship" was an act of trust and care, and "submission" was a joy and a privilege.

8

CRUCIFORM LORDSHIP

BUILDING WOOD FORTS WAS ONE OF MY favorite pastimes as a kid growing up. Honestly, I don't know how many I built. But they all had one thing in common: they were death traps.

I never planned any of them out beforehand. I didn't know what blueprints were, had no sketches, and no real idea of how it should be put together. My brother and I just started hammering boards or stacking clear-cut logs in the forest near our house.

Every one of those makeshift forts was an ER visit waiting to happen. One in particular was seven feet tall, made of wood stacked Lincoln-log style. After our "masterpiece" was finished, my brother and I stepped back in pride, only to realize we'd forgotten to construct a door. Our brilliant solution? Dig a tunnel through the foundation, which, of course, undermined the whole structure. The next day, we brought our neighbor friends back with us to see our triumph, only to find 400 pounds of logs collapsed in the exact spot we'd been playing. So naturally, we built it again.

Is a home built by piling lumber and bricks on the ground randomly? Can a home stand if the foundation is undermined? Or is a solid home built by design and with purpose? The same is true of our spiritual homes. Without foundation and structure, without leadership and direction, we don't flourish; we struggle and languish.

Understanding Biblical Submission

The concept of male headship is found in a variety of NT texts, both explicitly and implicitly. Beyond Ephesians 5, this pattern is woven throughout the apostolic writings. In 1 Corinthians 11:3, Paul establishes a clear order of authority: "But I want you to understand that the head of every man is Christ, the head of a wife is her husband, and the head of Christ is God." This passage reveals headship as both relational and functional. Just as Christ voluntarily submits to the Father while remaining equal in nature to Him, so the wife submits to her husband while maintaining her status as an equal image-bearer.

The principle appears again in Colossians 3:18–19, where wives are called to submit "as is fitting in the Lord," while husbands are commanded to love and not be harsh. Even in passages that don't explicitly use headship language, the pattern is strongly implied, such as in 1 Peter 3:1–7. Wives are called to respectful submission and husbands to understanding leadership. The same principle appears in Titus 2:3–5. Older women are to teach what accords with sound doctrine and train younger women in faithfulness, orderliness, and submission to their husbands, "that the word of God may not be reviled."

This consistent apostolic witness suggests that male headship in marriage and in ministry is a fundamental aspect of God's design for the family, rooted in creation and ultimately pointing to the relationship between Christ and His Church. But what exactly does it mean to "submit" to someone's leadership?

What About Mutual Submission?

Our egalitarian friends often point to Paul's command for "mutual submission" in Ephesians 5:21. Indeed, Paul does call believers to "submit to one another," but we must understand this within his broader theology of societal structure and authority. The Greek *hypotassō* means "to be subject to" or "to place oneself under," not merely to show mutual respect or service. Paul consistently calls for humility and service among all ranks (Phil 2:3–4).

However, if "mutual submission" meant that every believer submits to every other believer in identical and interchangeable ways, then all meaningful distinctions of role would collapse. Parents would be subject to their children, professors to their students, and leaders to those they are called to lead. Even Christ would be subject to the church. But the context makes clear that Paul does not envision a flattening of authority structures. His call to mutual submission does not erase ordered relationships or functions; it merely governs how they are exercised. Mutual submission, then, describes the spirit of humility that should permeate every Christian relationship, not the erasure of God-ordained roles.

As a house requires structure to stand, so the church and family flourish when organized according to God's design, where loving headship and responsive submission reflect the unity and beauty of Christ's body.

A License to Crush Others?

But were an abuser to twist these passages into a warrant for heavy-handed rule, Paul makes plain that Christ's leadership is *cruciform lordship*: it is leadership in the shape of Jesus' sacrificial love on the cross.

For example, the parents oversee the family, but this isn't a license to infuriate and exasperate their children, which ultimately drives them away from Christ and His church (Eph 6:1–4). That authority is exercised with the utmost care for the little ones in our charge. Likewise, servants are to obey their human masters with proper reverence and sincerity of heart, just as they would serve Christ (Eph 6:5–8). The indentured in Greco-Roman society were to take the posture of submission to those in positions of authority "as unto the Lord," expecting full repayment from Christ himself for their faithfulness when He returns.

And turning to the slaver, Paul says, "Masters, treat your servants the same way, without threatening them, because you know that both their Master and yours is in heaven, and there is no favoritism with him" (Eph 6:9). This is a radical claim indeed. Paul here states that the "master-servant" relationship is to be one in which authority is defined by benevolent care and conviviality. In that ancient context, the masters were to honor the slaves "in the same way," that is, realizing that the person in charge is ultimately answerable to Christ and will receive their just deserts from Him.

In all these relationships, Paul does not erase either personhood or the social order of his day but radically redefines both under Christ: both the one submitted and the "head" or leader are fellow servants of one Lord. Those in positions of authority are to take great care in their leadership because they will answer to Christ and be found liable should they lead in a manner unworthy of Him.

Summary

Let's take a brief survey of this unfolding submission as Paul outlines it in Ephesians:

- We are all privileged to submit to God the Father as Sovereign over all. Being under His "headship" is a high honor and is partly what it means to be a member of the image-bearing kind. We are quite literally living in a divine patriarchy, where God the Father is a generous, benevolent Lord.
- Christ voluntarily submitted to the Father in the incarnation to expose how we've misunderstood authority, showing that it is meant to be beautiful, sacrificial, and God-

honoring, not oppressive. Jesus then reclaims this creational design.

- The church is submitted to Christ, which is a high honor; that submission leads to social well-being, not shame or suppression of freedoms.

- The husband, in full submission to Christ and the Father, exercises God-honoring headship of the family. His submission to this command is cruciform stewardship, characterized by self-giving and self-sacrificial love for and leadership of those in his charge.

- The wife submits to her own husband as a glad and gracious response to God's beautiful, sovereign order in creation. Her submission is "in all things as unto the Lord." The same mindset of submission that we have to Christ, she is to have to her husband.

- The privilege of submission, as a posture of discipleship and apprenticeship to Jesus, is now open to women, no longer reserved for men only. Men now have the responsibility to lead wives and children in the instruction of the Lord, so that they, too, can lead others in the truth of the gospel.

Just as Christ submitted voluntarily to the Father (1 Cor 11:3), He has set that pattern for us all. We now turn briefly to answer a few more objections to this biblical view of headship and submission.

Does "Head" Mean "Source"?

We briefly noted above that egalitarians typically argue that Paul's use of the word "head" (*kephalē*) simply means "source," like the headwaters of a river. If translated so, then these passages do not affirm male leadership but merely male origin.

In fairness, it's true that in some classical Greek contexts, *kephalē* can mean "source" or "beginning," especially when referring to literal or metaphorical rivers. For example, Herodotus (Histories 4.91) uses *kephalē* to describe the "head" or "source" of the Tearus River. Similar uses are also found in other geographical descriptions.

Yet, it's also fair to point out that in other extra-biblical texts, this word unambiguously means "authority figure." So the word *kephalē* ("head") can mean either "source/origin" or "one in a position of governance." Sometimes the word carries both senses at once, as in 1 Corinthians 11, where Paul teaches that the woman came from man as her source/origin "For man was not made from woman, but woman from man" (1 Cor 11:8) and that she is to be under the man's headship "the head of a wife is her husband," 1 Cor 11:3, a truth symbolized by the head covering as a sign of "authority" (1 Cor 11:10). However, Paul's contexts resist reducing *kephalē* to merely meaning "source" for he consistently uses the term elsewhere to denote Christ's governing authority over the church (Eph 1:22–23; 5:23; Col 1:18), not simply His role as origin or wellspring. We observe the following:

Paul presents Christ not only as the source of the church's life but as the One who governs, nourishes, and directs her (Eph 1:22–23; Col 1:18). In Paul's letters, headship carries the sense of leadership. When he describes Christ's triumph over every power, he writes, "For God has put everything under his feet" (1 Cor 15:27). He then clarifies that the Father is not subjected to the Son, but that the Son is willingly subject to the Father (vv. 27–28). Christ reigns until every enemy, including death, is destroyed.

In these contexts, to reduce the concept of "head" to only "source" empties the metaphor of its force. The head gives life, sure, but it also *directs and governs* that life. Thus, when Paul says, "the husband is the head of the wife as Christ is the head of the church" (Eph 5:23), he isn't calling men to some vague notion of being merely a point of origin. He calls them to sacrificial, responsible leadership patterned after Jesus himself. This is self-giving love that seeks the family's highest good. The husband is not called to a vague servility, but to the God-given task of serving by leading and loving well in Christ.

What About Galatians 3:28?

But doesn't Paul erase all these so-called "cultural distinctions" when he writes to the Galatians, "There is no Jew or Greek, slave or free, *male and female*, for you are all one in Christ Jesus" (Gal 3:28, emphasis added)? At first glance, that seems to settle it. But this interpretation would also contradict everything Paul says about order and roles in the household codes of Ephesians 5 and Colossians 3. But when we take a closer look at the context of Galatians, it's clear that Paul isn't erasing all gender or social distinctions.

Backing up a bit in chapter 3, Paul states, "For through faith you are all sons of God in Christ Jesus" (Gal 3:26). Paul stresses that Jews and Gentiles are *both included in God's covenant family* by faith. This directly addresses the problem in Galatia of a faction of Pharisaic Christians from Jerusalem known as the "Judaizers" who were attempting to reconvert the Gentile Christians to Judaism. Apparently, they insisted that believers be circumcised, observe dietary laws and special holidays such as the Sabbath and Jewish high festivals (Passover, Day of Atonement, Pentecost, etc.). The term "sons" in 3:26 is a legal inheritance title in the Roman world. In most cases, only sons could inherit the father's property and estate. Here, Paul emphasizes that all Gentiles are now included with full "sonship" as inheritors of God's promises.

And he reminds them that they received this inheritance *by faith* when they received the Holy Spirit, not by observing these marks of Judaism through Torah observance. In other words, believing Gentiles are now full members of the covenant family of God by grace through faith and not by Judaic works of the law.

He continues, "For those of you who were baptized into Christ have been clothed with Christ" (Gal 3:27). This refers to Spirit-wrought incorporation into Christ—the new covenant marker of belonging. Circumcision, Sabbath, and kosher laws no longer define the covenant community; union with Christ does.

Now, this is not an *erasure of all distinctions* but a transformation of one's *fundamental identity*. His point is not that these creational distinctions have all been erased, but that none of them *determine one's status as a "son of God"* or an inheritor of the promises. The ground is level at the foot of the cross. There are no more racial barriers between Jews and Greeks, no more social barriers between slave and free, and no more sex-based barriers between male or female because "If you belong to Christ, then you are Abraham's seed, heirs according to the promise" (Gal 3:29). The point is that God shows no favoritism between these groups *for salvation*.

The reason this passage doesn't contradict Paul's teaching in Ephesians 5 and Colossians 3 about household order and godly hierarchy is that the contexts are entirely different. In Galatians, Paul is addressing the question, "Who belongs to God's covenant family?" In Ephesians and Colossians, he is concerned with, "How is that family to live and function together?" Two different questions, two distinct contexts—neither cancels out the other.

Others contend that if submission is desirable and therefore prescribed by Paul, it must be symmetrical rather than gender-specific. But beauty does not require symmetry in application. A symphony is beautiful not because every instrument plays the same notes, but because each contributes its distinct role to the overall unified score.

Did Paul Accommodate the Patriarchy?

Egalitarians frequently claim that Paul was merely accommodating patriarchal culture, using headship as an evangelistic strategy, a way to make the gospel culturally relevant and therefore palatable to Greco-Roman sensibilities. However, this argument confuses categories in a way that ultimately undermines its own effectiveness.

Paul indeed adapts in morally neutral matters, what theologians call *adiaphora* or "indifferent things." For example, he circumcises Timothy (Acts 16:3) but not Titus (Gal 2:3). He eats or abstains from certain foods depending on his audience (1 Cor 8–10; Rom 14:1–23). He becomes "all things to all people" (1 Cor 9:19–23), adapting his approach to suit the situation. In each case, however, these are neutral matters.

But as the egalitarian argument goes, we should also categorize "headship" into this "flex" or neutral category as a mere evangelization strategy for a patriarchal society. Once we are no longer in such a world (they argue), we can quickly disregard Paul's instructions on these archaisms.

But the problem with this thinking should be clear. If headship is inherently oppressive and unjust, as egalitarians argue, then Paul wasn't just accommodating culture; he was prescribing sin as an evangelistic strategy. Nowhere in his letters does he sanctify sinful practices for the sake of mission. He openly opposed prostitution, theft, cheating, factionalism, mistreatment of slaves, and every form of injustice. He didn't tell the Corinthians, "Keep visiting the temple prostitutes for now so that you may win a hearing with Corinthian pimps."

He didn't tell masters to keep beating their slaves as a temporary measure so that eventually they could win other slave owners to the gospel. When Paul encountered sin, he consistently denounced it and never adopted it as a means to accomplish anything for God. And if male leadership is inherently sinful, then why think Paul would adopt or appeal to this sinful enterprise as an evangelistic strategy?

We must say in response that creation norms are not culturally negotiable. They precede and transcend every human society. Structure is the framework for relational *shalom*. God desires His creatures to live in right relationship with Him and one another. And that relational harmony often does require a godly structural hierarchy.

Affirming Women Without Flattening Roles

Egalitarians rightly point out that Paul affirmed women in significant ministry. As noted previously, Priscilla instructed Apollos (Acts 18:26), Phoebe served as a deacon (Rom 16:1), Junia was "outstanding among the apostles" (Rom 16:7), and women prayed and prophesied in the church (1 Cor 11:5). These are real affirmations.

But affirmation in some roles does not erase the need to distinguish others. Not all men qualify as apostles, prophets, evangelists, or pastor-teachers. This is precisely Paul's point when he insists that God accomplishes his unified purposes through a diversity of Spiritual gifts, "And there are different activities, but the same God works all of them in each person" (1 Cor 12:6), and again, "Are all apostles? Are all prophets? Are all teachers?" We are coequal members of Christ's body, but with a variety of gifts that complement the whole.

This would apply to the women whom Jesus clearly entrusted as the first witnesses of the resurrection. A high privilege indeed. And certainly an act of elevating women for first-century readers of the gospel accounts. But so far as we know, none were appointed among the Twelve apostles who were promised governing thrones in God's new economy (Luke 22:28–30). Paul, though championing women coworkers, still restricted elder-teaching authority to men, and grounded that in creation, not culture.

Jesus and the Twelve

Another common objection runs like this: Jesus elevated women in radical ways; therefore, He must have intended to erase headship entirely. No doubt (as we have argued), Jesus certainly dignified women in a culture that often marginalized them. He taught women as disciples (Luke 10:38–42), defended them from religious exploitation (Mark

12:40), allowed them to travel with His ministry team (Luke 8:1–3), and commissioned them as the first witnesses of His resurrection (John 20:11–18). We agree that Jesus shattered cultural prejudices at every turn. But this argument actually works *against the egalitarian case* for the following reasons.

First, if Jesus intended to abolish male headship and leadership as a relic of patriarchalism, why did He deliberately avoid appointing women as Apostles? This was no concession to cultural pressure. Jesus often defied cultural norms when they conflicted with God's will. He touched lepers, ate with tax collectors, and rebuked religious leaders to their faces. He spoke alone with the Samaritan woman at the well (John 4), leaving His own male disciples shocked. He accepted financial support from women and welcomed them into His traveling ministry—both radical acts in that culture (Luke 8:1–3). He wasn't timid about confronting injustice.

Yet when it came to establishing the foundational leadership of His church, the apostolic office that would carry unique governing authority (Matt 19:28; Rev. 21:14), He chose twelve men and appointed no women among the Twelve. If male leadership were inherently sinful and domineering, Jesus had countless opportunities to signal its abolition by appointing women to positions of authority within his inner circle among the Twelve. He didn't.

Second, when Jesus teaches on marriage in Matthew 19:4–6, He doesn't revise or abolish the creational pattern. Instead, he reiterates it, "He who created them from the beginning made them male and female." He then upholds male initiative to start a family, "A man shall leave his father and mother and hold fast to his wife." Jesus reaffirms marriage in the created order, echoing the structure Paul later builds upon.

To argue that Jesus implicitly abolished headship through His treatment of women would require us to believe that this supposed revolution was so subtle that He failed to pass it on to Peter, the Twelve, or Paul. Peter, who boldly confronted the Judaizers over circumcision (Acts 15), supposedly missed it. Paul, who publicly rebuked Peter to his face for hobnobbing with a Jewish faction (Gal 2:11), supposedly capitulated to patriarchal norms when writing to Timothy and the Ephesians. John, who personally witnessed Jesus' radical inclusion of women (a detail central to his Gospel), somehow failed to grasp its supposed implications when composing his letters. The egalitarian reading must therefore stretch from the Bible's clear affirmation of women in ministry (a general observation) to an assumption of their eligibility for the pastoral office (a specific claim), a leap Scripture itself never makes.

The apostles who walked with Jesus, who saw Him elevate women, heard Him teach, and witnessed His resurrection, are the very ones who later affirm male headship in the home and church. They didn't see a contradiction because there isn't one. Jesus dignified women without erasing the very distinctions that He ordained in creation. We're expected to believe that the Apostles, who so boldly confronted genuine patriarchal abuses—forbidding men to divorce wives on a whim (Matt 19:3–9), commanding husbands to love sacrificially (Eph. 5:25–28), insisting that women are co-heirs of grace (1 Pet 3:7)—somehow mysteriously caved to cultural pressure on the subject of headship and creational order in the home. For what? For the sake of evangelism?

The Divine Authority of 1 Timothy

Another typical refrain from the egalitarian camp is that Paul's command, "I do not permit a woman to teach or to exercise authority over a man" (1 Tim 2:12), is merely his opinion rather than an inspired, universal restriction. As noted in more detail in the previous chapters, his limitation was just a temporary concession for a raging crisis in Ephesus at the time (something about uneducated women causing problems, etc.). So, Paul's instructions here, they argue, don't rise to the level of authoritative, universally binding Scripture. This was Paul's situational advice, not the Lord's divine command.

But this argument is weakened when we consider the letter as a whole. Paul begins with a direct claim to divine authority: "Paul, an apostle of Christ Jesus *by command of God our Savior*" (1 Tim 1:1). This doesn't look like a casual, personal greeting. Instead, Paul establishes that he writes not as a private individual dispensing sage advice or waxing eloquent with sapiential maxims, but as Christ's commissioned representative, delivering authoritative instruction.

In fact, throughout the letter, Paul repeatedly underscores the theological weightiness of his own instruction. He charges Timothy "as I urged you when I was going to Macedonia to command certain people not to teach false doctrine" (1 Tim 1:3). He gives Timothy "this charge" in accordance with prophecies made about him (1 Tim 1:18). He speaks of "the command of our Savior" (1 Tim 1:1) and writes so that Timothy will know "how one ought to behave in the household of God" (1 Tim 3:15). Later, he adjures his protege "in the presence of God and of Christ Jesus and of the elect angels" to keep these instructions (1 Tim 5:21) and again charges him "in the presence of God, who gives life to all things, and of Christ Jesus" (1 Tim 6:13). He even claims direct prophetic authority, "Now the Spirit expressly says..." (1 Tim 4:1). Unlike the Corinthian correspondence (1 Cor 7), he gives no indication that he is speaking to Timothy as a matter of mere wisdom without a direct command from God. Throughout the book, his tone carries the weight of divine authority.

Furthermore, Paul explicitly tells Timothy to guard "what has been entrusted to you" (1 Tim 6:20), the deposit of apostolic teaching. There's no indication here that he's passing along advice for navigating Ephesian social dynamics. Frankly, to reduce these imperatives to cultural accommodation is to undermine the doctrine of inspiration itself.

Furthermore, if Paul's clear, unqualified commands rooted in creation can be dismissed as culturally conditioned, then what in Scripture can't or shouldn't be? Where do we draw the line? The commands against sexual immorality? Greed? Slander? Or for children to obey their parents? Paul uses the same authoritative tone throughout. If we can set aside 1 Timothy 2:12 as "just cultural," we've opened the door to dismissing anything we find uncomfortable or personally objectionable in Scripture. Just consider that people seldom leap into doctrinal ruin; they drift toward it, step by subtle step, down the slippery slope, surrendering truth one concession at a time. For that reason, we should resist taking such a view.

Saved Through Childbearing

Paul concludes this section (1 Tim 2:11–15) with a puzzling statement that seems, at first, to come out of nowhere: "But she will be saved through childbearing—if they continue in faith, love, and holiness, with good sense" (1 Tim 2:15). Egalitarians often argue that since this verse appears culturally bound or even confusing, it must indicate that Paul's earlier restriction on women teaching or exercising authority addressed a specific societal catastrophe rather than a universal principle. In other words, if we don't treat the "childbearing" verse (v. 15) as a timeless doctrine (they argue), why should we treat the teaching restriction two verses earlier (v. 12) as one? The two verses are linked, so they must both be cultural accommodations. But this logic fails on multiple levels.

First, let's acknowledge the difficulty: "Saved (Greek *sōzō*) through childbearing" is indeed a challenging phrase, and Christian interpreters have wrestled with it for centuries. But the mere difficulty in interpreting the phrase does not automatically equate to a "cultural" or culturally conditioned lens for Paul. Scripture contains many hard sayings that remain authoritative and transcultural. The question isn't whether a text is difficult, but whether it's grounded in a universally applied truth or a temporary circumstance.

Paul grounds his restriction on women teaching or exercising authority in the garden, before any fallen culture existed. Verse 15, by contrast, speaks to a consequence of the Fall and how Christian women can endure it with faith and hope.

So what does this puzzling phrase, "saved through childbearing," mean? The Greek word *sōzō* ("to save") carries a range of meanings depending on the context of any given passage. It often refers to spiritual salvation (Eph 2:8), but it can also denote physical deliverance from danger (Matt 8:25; Acts 27:20), healing from disease (Mark 5:23; Luke 8:48), or preservation through trials (Phil 1:19; 2 Tim 4:18). The term *sōzō* is flexible. Historically, this phrase in 1 Timothy 2:15 has been understood in three primary ways.

Option 1: Eve is saved through "the" promised Child (Gen 3:15), Christ: Some connect it to Eve's promise of a "seed" who would crush the serpent (Gen. 3:15), arguing that Christ's birth, as the child of the woman, brings salvation to humanity. However, Paul isn't discussing humanity's salvation through Christ's birth, but rather *Eve's* salvation in solidarity with womankind, not humankind.

Option 2: Saved From Childbearing Mortality: Some early church bishops and pastors (Patristics) suggested that Christian women would be delivered safely *through the process* of childbirth itself, that God would preserve them from the physical dangers of labor, the result of her judgment in the Fall (Gen 3:16). But this interpretation doesn't match Paul's context either. Moreover, Christian women still die in childbirth. If Paul meant guaranteed physical preservation, the promise has demonstrably failed throughout church history.

Option 3: Saved from "Gendercide": The third interpretation is the most compelling—women will be delivered from a culture that devalues them. By embracing their God-given calling to bear and nurture life, rather than abandoning it or capitulating to a society that devalues motherhood, women are "rescued" or saved from this ongoing assault on womanhood itself.

Consider the context. The patron deity of Ephesus was Artemis, the virgin goddess of fertility, which often led to female celibacy. Combine that with the wider abhorrent Greco-Roman practice of exposing or killing infant girls (infanticide), and you have an anti-family ethos that predictably eroded the culture's demographic future. Women were often viewed as expendable, valued primarily for their utility. Not to mention the fact that childbearing itself could be dangerous before the advent of modern medicine.[1]

Many nations today should follow Paul's instructions and listen to their own statisticians. The breakeven replacement rate for every nation is 2.1 children. Many Western and Asian countries are nowhere near that. The UK is at 1.44. Japan just notched a record-low at 1.14. China is near 1.15. Germany sits around 1.35, Russia about 1.41, and South Korea is hovering near demographic collapse at about 0.75. Run those numbers forward, and you don't get a hopeful future; you get fewer workers, smaller consumer and tax bases, and thinner draft pools. Policies that depress and discourage family formation are quite literally suicidal to a nation's interests.

And it's not just nation-states; it's happening in churches, too. Just look at the pews. When a church stops making disciples, it starts managing decline. If the nursery goes quiet and the baptistry is dry, eventually the lights go off and the doors close permanently. Church buildings that once held the faithful for a century or more are now being converted to black-box theaters, condos, or community arts centers.

It is against this cultural and cultic assault on family and reproduction that Paul prioritizes a creational design for the Ephesians. Paul affirms that in Christ, women are preserved, protected, and honored through the very thing that pagan culture despised and disposed of. We may not pay homage to Artemis in literal temples today, but modern people are still worshiping this false devil god through abortive and anti-family policies.

By contrast, Christian communities valued traditional Jewish roles for men and women. They didn't throw infants away like trash, especially their girls. They cared for women in childbirth. They saw motherhood not as a curse or as something to be liberated from, but as a high calling worthy of honor. They charged their men to step up and teach the church as proper and honored authority figures. Far from a cultural accommodation, Paul's instruction is a *universal correction* to the heathen's devaluation of women and the miracle of reproduction. For this alone will save and preserve them. And in so doing, they will save and preserve the human race from annihilation.

SUMMARY

THE CRISIS FACING THE CHURCH TODAY is not a simple one. In many places, Christian men have quietly withdrawn from the responsibilities God had originally entrusted to them. All this while our culture has led men into sin and denied our need for male leadership.

Too often, the church has followed the world's example.

When men shrink back from their calling, families and congregations drift without steady direction. Women then carry more than they were ever meant to carry—shouldering both their own callings while feeling the weight of absent leadership. Pushing against the emasculated tide of American life, many long to rediscover the blessing of faithful, godly men who will lead and love like Jesus. This book has sought to sketch a better way.

Chapter 1 identified the problem: male disengagement born of role confusion—fatherlessness, prolonged adolescence, and a feminized church culture are not optimal in the church. The solution requires recovering a biblical vision where both men and women flourish in their God-given callings.

Chapter 2 established the foundation: from the beginning, men and women stand equal as image-bearers of God, equally resourced, equally accountable, and equally guilty before Him. The woman is not the man's slave, but a strong and suitable counterpart pulled from his side to complete what he alone could not accomplish. Together they form one flesh, one priesthood, two halves of a whole life ordained to fill, subdue, and sanctify the earth for God's glory.

Chapter 3 revealed that within this equality exists a divinely sanctioned order. Adam was formed first, called first, commanded first, and first held accountable for what transpired in their home. This "firstness" is not arbitrary but reflects God's deliberate design in nature and marriage. Adam's priority is not a crown of privilege but a mantle of responsibility and a sacred trust.

Chapter 4 showed how the Fall corrupted God's good order. The curse struck at the junction of each partner's strengths: the woman's desire twisted into rivalry for control, the man's leadership perverted into domination or passivity. What was meant to be harmony became a contest of wills. Yet Jesus does not abolish the need for male leadership;

He redeems it, transforming tyranny into cruciform lordship patterned after the self-giving love of the cross. And the natural response to that godly leadership is the wife and children's glad and joyful submission and respect.

Chapter 5 stressed that Scripture consistently affirms women in vital ministry roles. From Deborah to Phoebe, from the daughters of Philip to Priscilla, women prophesied, taught, led, and pioneered the gospel mission. Their contributions were essential in the life of the early church that Christ founded. The promise of Pentecost required it: the world cannot know Christ has come unless our daughters also prophesy and minister the gospel in the power of the Holy Spirit. A good church unleashes that potential by encouraging and releasing women to serve in the areas of their spiritual gifts.

In Chapter 6, we addressed the so-called "problem passages" which appear to promote women's subjugation in the Church through "silence" in Corinth. We discovered that far from silencing women universally, Paul was inviting uneducated women into the privilege of learning Christ's teaching. The command for silence was not suppression but the pathway to discipleship and ministry. In contrast to the suppression of women in Greco-Roman society, the Christian Church advocated education and service through the spiritual gifts of all its members.

Chapter 7 directly addressed another problematic text in 1 Timothy 2, where Paul restricts the office of elder-teacher to qualified men. We discovered that this restriction, while applicable to the Ephesian crisis, *wasn't rooted in Ephesian culture or in a temporary crisis,* but in creation itself, for "Adam was formed first, then Eve." We saw that Paul's appeal to Genesis in this regard was not an *ad hoc* analogy he created on the fly for illustrative purposes, but a deep Judeo-Christian theological principle of *ordo creationis,* the order of creation that precedes and transcends human societal norms. This order is woven into the fabric of creation itself. To dismiss Paul's framing in Genesis is to de-contextualize Paul, undermining his entire theological method.

Chapter 8 brought the vision full circle: biblical headship is cruciform lordship—leadership shaped by the cross. Husbands are called to love as Christ loved the church in sacrificial, sanctifying leadership. Wives respond not in cowering compliance but in glad partnership with a man whose leadership is patterned after Christ's example.

The biblical vision is clear: men and women are equal in dignity, distinct in function, and unified in mission. When men abdicate, everyone suffers. When women are sidelined or forced into inappropriate leadership roles, the church is adversely affected. But when both embrace their callings—men leading with cross-shaped love, women serving as an added strength in the body, the gospel advances, families flourish, and God's image is on full display for all to see. This is the world God intended. This is the vision we must recover. Neither tyrants running little fiefdoms, nor token wives who sit idly by while men do all the praying, giving, serving, and ministering. In a wayward world starving for this creational design, this is the vision worth recovering: men who lead as Christ bled, and women who thrive under their care and guidance.

Endnotes

Chapter 1: Where Two Horizons Meet

1. For the case for toxic masculinity see Clementine Ford, *Boys Will Be Boys: Power, Patriarchy and Toxic Masculinity* (Melbourne: Allen & Unwin, 2018); for the case against it see Nancy R. Pearcey, *The Toxic War on Masculinity: How Christianity Reconciles the Sexes* (Ada, MI: Baker, 2023); Voddie Baucham, *What He Must Be ... If He Wants to Marry My Daughter* (Wheaton, IL: Crossway, 2009); Voddie Baucham, *Family Shepherds: Calling and Equipping Men to Lead Their Homes* (Wheaton, IL: Crossway, 2011); Sean McDowell and Scott Rae, "Truth and Toxic Masculinity," *Think Biblically* (Biola University, August 3, 2023).

2. See Allen J. Beck, Susan A. Kline, and Lawrence A. Greenfeld, *Survey of Youth in Custody, 1987* (Washington, DC: U.S. Department of Justice, Bureau of Justice Statistics, September 1988), NCJ-113365; Jack Brewer, "Fatherlessness and Crime," fact sheet, Center for Opportunity Now, America First Policy Institute, August 25, 2022; Federal Reserve Bank of St. Louis, "Poverty Status of Families by Type of Family," *FRED* release tables (from "Income and Poverty in the United States," 2024), accessed February 26, 2026; Iryna Culpin, Hein Heuvelman, Dheeraj Rai, Rebecca M. Pearson, Carol Joinson, Jon Heron, Jonathan Evans, and Alex S. F. Kwong, "Father absence and trajectories of offspring mental health across adolescence and young adulthood: Findings from a UK-birth cohort," *Journal of Affective Disorders* 314 (October 1, 2022): 150–159,

doi:10.1016/j.jad.2022.07.016; Lindsay M. Monte, "The Two Extremes of Fatherhood," *America Counts*, U.S. Census Bureau, November 5, 2019.

3. Leonard Sax, *Boys Adrift: The Five Factors Driving the Growing Epidemic of Unmotivated Boys and Underachieving Young Men* (New York: Basic Books, 2007). The main drivers of male disengagement are generally considered to be: (1) Father Absence (in the home, and arguably from culture at large): In the US, approximately 25% of children live in homes with no father figure at all. Fatherlessness contributes to higher incidents of poverty and behavioral problems, resulting in an increased risk of cognitive, social, and emotional difficulties, leading to narcissistic or abusive behavior. (2) Unemployment or Underemployment: Men in lower-income families typically face higher levels of stress, suppressed anger, and addiction, leading to behavioral problems and father absence. (3) Cultural Abandonment: The highly feminized and emasculating shift in social norms has led men to feel unwanted and unnecessary.

4. The broader cultural landscape has shifted dramatically in recent decades. As of 2024, women constitute 56% of law school students, 77% of public school teachers, 51% of the global teaching workforce, and earn the majority of doctoral degrees. Men account for only 25% of recipients of Ph. D.s in psychology, and the publishing industry is 71% female. Yet male participation in certain trades, such as that of bricklaying, remains near 100%. These statistics reflect unprecedented educational and professional access for women. However, they also indicate that traditional models of male leadership now operate in a cultural

context that views such patterns with suspicion or outright hostility, making the recovery of biblical complementarianism more urgent and increasingly countercultural.

5. For further reading, see Ronald W. Pierce, Cynthia Long Westfall, and Christa L. McKirland, eds., *Discovering Biblical Equality: Biblical, Theological, Cultural, and Practical Perspectives*, 3rd ed. (Downers Grove, IL: IVP Academic, 2021); Craig S. Keener, Paul, *Women, and Wives: Marriage and Women's Ministry in the Letters of Paul* (Grand Rapids: Baker Academic, 1992); John Piper and Wayne Grudem, eds., *Recovering Biblical Manhood and Womanhood: A Response to Evangelical Feminism* (Wheaton, IL: Crossway, 1991); Andreas J. Köstenberger and Thomas R. Schreiner, eds., *Women in the Church: An Interpretation and Application of 1 Timothy 2:9–15*, 3rd ed. (Wheaton, IL: Crossway, 2016).

Chapter 2. Neither Tyrants nor Tokens

1. Gerhard F. Hasel, "Equality from the Start: Woman in the Creation Story," *Spectrum* 7, no. 2 (1975): 21–28.

2. See the Egyptian creation myths of Atum and Nut; the Mesopotamian accounts of the Eridu Genesis involving An, Enlil, Enki, and Nintur; the narrative of Enki and Ninmah; and the Babylonian Enuma Elish concerning Tiamat, Apsu, and Marduk, in which humans are little more than slaves to the gods. For discussion, see Loren R. Fisher, "Creation at Ugarit and in the Old Testament," *Vetus Testamentum* 15 (1965): 313–24; Christopher B. Hays, *Hidden Riches: A Sourcebook for the Comparative Study of the Hebrew Bible and the Ancient Near East* (Louisville, KY: Westminster

John Knox, 2014); John Walton, *Genesis 1 as Ancient Cosmology* (Winona Lake, IN: Eisenbrauns, 2011).

Chapter 3. The Privilege and the Mantle

1. Mark, Joshua J. "Enuma Elish—The Babylonian Epic of Creation—Full Text." World History Enclyclopedia. In fact, their combat was thought to literally form the natural world, as Tiamat's watery corpse became the "heavens and earth," storms, and various floods associated with her fury and resistance before her defeat. See also Mark S. Smith, *The Early History of God: Yahweh and the Other Deities in Ancient Israel* (Grand Rapids: Eerdmans, 2002), 12–15; Stephanie Dalley, *Myths from Mesopotamia: Creation, the Flood, Gilgamesh, and Others*, rev. ed. (Oxford: Oxford University Press, 2000), 45–47; John Day, *Yahweh and the Gods and Goddesses of Canaan* (JSOTSS 265; Sheffield: Sheffield Academic Press, 2000).)

2. Mitka R. Golub, "What's in a Name? Personal Names in Ancient Israel and Judah," *BAR* 46, no. 2 (2020): 28–35; "Personal Names and Name Giving in the ancient Near East," *JAOS* 103, no. 1 (1983): 11–18; D. Stuart, "Names, Proper," in *ISBE Revised*, ed. Geoffrey W. Bromiley (Eerdmans, 1979–1988), 3:485; David Witthoff, ed., *The Lexham Cultural Ontology Glossary* (Bellingham, WA: Lexham Press, 2014).

3. Grammatically, the Shema שְׁמַע (*shema*, "hear!") is addressed to Israel as a covenant whole, personified as a single entity. Hebrew consistently uses masculine singular forms when addressing the nation as "Israel." Later in Deut 11:18–19 and Deut 32:46, Moses applies these same commands more concretely to "fathers" (אֲבוֹתֵיכֶם, ʾ*avotekem*) as those who must bind the law on

their hearts and teach it diligently to their children. Likewise, the command to "Bind them as a sign on your hand" (v. 8) was interpreted to refer to fathers.

4. Linda L. Belleville, "Women in Ministry: An Egalitarian Perspective," in *Two Views on Women in Ministry*, ed. James R. Beck and Stanley N. Gundry, rev. ed. (Grand Rapids, MI: Zondervan, 2005), 45.

Chapter 4. Domination and Desire

1. Brown, Francis, Samuel Rolles Driver, and Charles Augustus Briggs. *A Hebrew and English Lexicon of the Old Testament* (Oxford: Clarendon Press, 1906).

2. For further reading on the biological distinctions between men and women as they relate to various jobs and sports see Sophia Zhuang, "Men and Women Are Physiologically Unequal: An Equal Research Emphasis," *Yale Scientific Magazine*, November 28, 2020; Pew Research Center, "How Americans See Differences Between Men and Women," *Pew Research Center*, October 17, 2024.

Chapter 5. Unless Our Daughters Also Prophesy

1. Patrick W. Skehan and Alexander A. Di Lella, *The Wisdom of Ben Sira*, AB 39 (Garden City, NY: Doubleday, 1987); *The Babylonian Talmud*, ed. Isidore Epstein (London: Soncino Press, 1935–1952); *The Midrash Rabbah*, trans. H. Freedman and Maurice Simon, 10 vols. (London: Soncino Press, 1939).

2. Brenda Longfellow, "Female Patrons and Honorific Statues in Pompeii," *Memoirs of the American Academy in Rome* 59/60 (2014/2015): 81–101; David A. deSilva, "Patronage," *DNTB*, *A Compendium of Contemporary*

Biblical Scholarship (Downers Grove, IL: InterVarsity Press, 2000), 770; Andrew Wallace-Hadrill, "Patronage in Roman Society: From Republic to Empire," in *Patronage in Ancient Society*, ed. Andrew Wallace-Hadrill, Leicester-Nottingham Studies in Ancient Society 1 (London: Routledge, 1989), 63–87; Barbara K. Gold, "Patronage and the Elegists: Social Reality or Literary Construction?" *Classical World* 85, no. 2 (1991): 129–142; Glenys Davies, "Portrait Statues as Models for Gender Roles in Roman Society," MAAR, *Supplementary* 7 (2008): 207–220.

3. BDAG, s.v. "Ἰουνία, ας, ἡ." Junia is a common feminine proper name, and there are no Greek manuscripts with the masculine "Junias." This name appears frequently in Roman inscriptions throughout the Roman Empire and is found in all social classes. Some have attempted to translate ἐν τοῖς ἀποστόλοις as "one who is honored by [among] the apostles," but this construction is not supported by the phrase ἐν τοῖς (*en tois*) in other contexts. When Luke records Jesus saying, "the greatest among you" (Luke 22:26), He refers to individuals within the group of disciples. Jesus refers to John as "among those born of women" (Matt 11:11); John states that the Word became flesh and "dwelt among us" (John 1:14); speaking of Judas, Peter states that he was counted "among us" (Acts 1:17); Paul describes the Philippians as ones who "shine as lights among the world" (Phil 2:15); "leaders among the brothers" (Acts 15:22); "whoever wants to become great among you" (Matt 20:26). In each of these NT contexts, it means "one from among" a group. Considering these examples, ἐν τοῖς ἀποστόλοις (*en tois apostolois*, "among the apostles") in Romans 16:7

is most naturally read as situating Andronicus and Junia within the group of apostles rather than as individuals outside the group merely honored *among* those in the group. The preposition ἐν consistently conveys inclusion or participation in the group when paired with a collective noun such as "apostles."

4. Paul also gives instructions regarding female deacons in 1 Timothy 3. In 1 Timothy 3:11, Paul uses the Greek word γυναῖκας (*gynaikas*), the plural form of γυνή (*gynē*), meaning "woman" or "wife." The verse reads: ὡσαύτως γυναῖκας σεμνάς, μὴ διαβόλους, νηφαλίους, πιστὰς ἐν πᾶσιν ("Likewise, women must be worthy of respect, not slanderers, self-controlled, faithful in everything"). If Paul intended this verse to refer only to the "wives" of deacons, why would he not apply the same standard to the wives of elders (vv. 1–7)? Moreover, the word "likewise" (ὡσαύτως) introduces a new category or group, as it does in verse 8 when introducing deacons, suggesting that Paul here refers to *female deacons*, not wives. Furthermore, no possessive modifier ("their") appears with *gynaikas*. Thus, this passage is best understood as referring to the *women*—female deaconesses—who regularly ministered in the congregation.

Chapter 6. Not a God of Disorder

1. Because Greek had no punctuation marks, the phrase "as in all the churches of the saints" (1 Cor 14:33) can go with the previous clause, which would render it: "God is not a God of disorder [as in all the churches of the saints]." In this case, there is no universal prohibition against women "speaking" in church. However, even if the phrase begins the

following paragraph, "[As in all the churches of the saints,] women are to remain silent," Paul's standard would still apply universally to any church where women remained largely uneducated and lacked discipleship training.

2. As I have argued elsewhere, what we call "literacy" (the ability to read and write) was most likely thought of as grapho-literacy possessed by scribal elites, in contrast to other acceptable ancient modes of "reading" which included oral-literacy (verbal recall and fluidity with texts), aural literacy (a hearing-based education). See Jeff S. Kennedy, *A Prophet Mighty in Deed and Word: Jesus' Subversive Reading of the Isaian Jubilee in Luke 4:16–30* (Eugene, OR: Pickwick Publications, 2022).

3. Plutarch, "On Listening to Lectures (De audiendo) 4.1," in *Moralia*, vol. 1, trans. F. C. Babbitt, LCL 197 (Cambridge, MA: Harvard University Press, 1927), 214–15; Plutarch [Pseudo-], "On the Education of Children (De liberis educandis) 10–11," in *Moralia*, vol. 1, trans. F. C. Babbitt, LCL 197 (Cambridge, MA: Harvard University Press, 1927); Lucian of Samosata, "The Parasite," §49, in *Lucian*, vol. 3, trans. A. M. Harmon, LCL 130 (Cambridge, MA: Harvard University Press, 1921); Henry George Liddell, Robert Scott, and Henry Stuart Jones, *A Greek–English Lexicon*, 9th ed. (Oxford: Clarendon, 1940), s.v. "ὑποτάσσω" (citing Lucian, *De parasito* 49); Frederick William Danker, ed., *A Greek–English Lexicon of the New Testament and Other Early Christian Literature*, 3rd ed. (Chicago: University of Chicago Press, 2000), s.v. "ὑποτάσσω"; "ὑποταγή."

Chapter 7. Woven into the World

1. Philo of Alexandria, *On the Life of Moses* 2.154–55, in *Philo*, vol. 6, *On Abraham. On Joseph. On Moses*, trans. F. H. Colson, LCL 289 (Cambridge, MA: Harvard University Press, 1935); Flavius Josephus, *Jewish Antiquities* 4.40–41, in *Josephus*, vol. 2, *Jewish Antiquities, Books 4–6*, trans. H. St. J. Thackeray and Ralph Marcus, LCL 490 (Cambridge, MA: Harvard University Press, 1930); *Sirach* 50:20–21, in *A New English Translation of the Septuagint*, ed. Albert Pietersma and Benjamin G. Wright (Oxford: Oxford University Press, 2007).

2. Ronald W. Pierce, Rebecca Merrill Groothuis, and Gordon D. Fee, eds., *Discovering Biblical Equality: Complementarity without Hierarchy*, 2nd ed. (Downers Grove, IL: IVP Academic, 2005).

3. Some argue that Paul "affirmed slavery" in the first-century setting, and therefore his teaching on headship should be read as similarly bound to culture. But that charge misses the point. In Paul's world, slavery was not interchangeable with our modern notion of race-based chattel slavery. First, slaves in Rome had no alternate social structures to fall back on. When an economic downturn forced masters to release them, many starved or turned to theft for survival and subsequently were caught and crucified. Paul could not simply snap his fingers and invent a new employment structure. Second, while Roman slavery could be cruel, much of it functioned more like indentured servitude. It was the default system of labor in place of a marketplace wage economy. Many entered slavery to pay debts, acquire training, or gain a path to citizenship. It could be temporary, and

manumission was a common practice. Third, and most decisive, Paul redeems the category itself by applying it to Christian discipleship. "Having been set free from sin, you became enslaved to God" (Rom 6:22). And again, "The one called as a slave is the Lord's freedman; likewise, the free man is Christ's slave" (1 Cor 7:22). He even says, "I have made myself a slave to everyone, to win more people" (1 Cor 9:19). Far from degrading believers, this language dignifies them: servitude to Christ is true freedom, and servitude to others is gospel-shaped love. So, when Paul speaks of slavery, he is not propping up a corrupt institution but drawing on its redemptive potential. Just as submission is not humiliation but ordered devotion, so servitude to Christ and His church is not oppression but the pathway to salvation and edification of the church.

8. Cruciform Lordship

1. From the first century to now, churches have always been tempted to absorb cultural distortions of gender, whether over-feminization or hyper-masculinization, rather than living out the biblical complement. If the dominant cultural force in Ephesus was a goddess who denied the goodness of marriage and childbearing, then Paul's corrective in 1 Timothy is sharpened. Rather than suppressing women, Paul is rooting Christian discipleship in a counter-cultural embrace of God's design for men and women, including the dignity of marriage, family, and childbearing. See Sandra L. Glahn, *Nobody's Mother: Artemis of the Ephesians in Antiquity and the New Testament* (Downers Grove, IL: InterVarsity Press, 2023); Ann M. E. Haentjens, "Reflections on Female Infanticide in the

Greco-Roman World," *L'Antiquité Classique* 69 (2000): 261–64; Donald Engels, "The Problem of Female Infanticide in the Greco-Roman World," *Classical Philology* 75, no. 2 (1980): 112–20; M. Obladen, "From Right to Sin: Laws on Infanticide in Antiquity," Neonatology 109, no. 4 (2016): 252–61.

Bibliography

Baucham, Voddie T., Jr. *Family Shepherds: Calling and Equipping Men to Lead Their Homes*. Wheaton, IL: Crossway, 2011.

————. *What He Must Be...If He Wants to Marry My Daughter*. Wheaton, IL: Crossway, 2009.

Belleville, Linda L. "Women in Ministry: An Egalitarian Perspective." In *Two Views on Women in Ministry*, edited by James R. Beck and Stanley N. Gundry, rev. ed., 19–85. Grand Rapids, MI: Zondervan, 2005.

Blomberg, Craig L. "Women in Ministry: A Complementarian Perspective." In *Two Views on Women in Ministry*, edited by James R. Beck and Stanley N. Gundry, rev. ed., 111–158. Grand Rapids, MI: Zondervan, 2005.

Brown, Francis, S. R. Driver, and Charles A. Briggs. *A Hebrew and English Lexicon of the Old Testament*. Oxford: Clarendon Press, 1906.

Dalley, Stephanie, trans. *Myths from Mesopotamia: Creation, the Flood, Gilgamesh, and Others*. Rev. ed. Oxford: Oxford University Press, 2000.

Day, John. *Yahweh and the Gods and Goddesses of Canaan.* JSOTSup 265. Sheffield: Sheffield Academic Press, 2000.

deSilva, David A. "Patronage." In *Dictionary of New Testament Background,* edited by Craig A. Evans and Stanley E. Porter, 766–772. Downers Grove, IL: InterVarsity Press, 2000.

Davies, Glenys. "Portrait Statues as Models for Gender Roles in Roman Society." In *Role Models in the Roman World: Identity and Assimilation, Memoirs of the American Academy in Rome, Supplementary Volumes* 7, edited by Sinclair Bell and Inge Lyse Hansen, 207–220. Ann Arbor: University of Michigan Press, 2008.

Engels, Donald. "The Problem of Female Infanticide in the Greco-Roman World." *Classical Philology* 75, no. 2 (1980): 112–120.

Fisher, Loren R. "Creation at Ugarit and in the Old Testament." *Vetus Testamentum* 15 (1965): 313–324.

Ford, Clementine. *Boys Will Be Boys: Power, Patriarchy and Toxic Masculinity.* Melbourne: Allen & Unwin, 2018.

Glahn, Sandra L. *Nobody's Mother: Artemis of the Ephesians in Antiquity and the New Testament.* Downers Grove, IL: IVP Academic, 2023.

Gold, Barbara K. "Patronage and the Elegists: Social Reality or Literary Construction?" *Classical World* 85, no. 2 (1991): 129–142.

Golub, Mitka R. "What's in a Name? Personal Names in Ancient Israel and Judah." *BAR* 46, no. 2 (2020): 28–35.

Haentjens, Ann M. E. "Reflections on Female Infanticide in the Greco-Roman World." *L'Antiquité Classique* 69 (2000): 261–64.

Hasel, Gerhard F. "Equality from the Start: Woman in the Creation Story." *Spectrum* 7, no. 2 (1975): 21–28.

Hays, Christopher B. *Hidden Riches: A Sourcebook for the Comparative Study of the Hebrew Bible and Ancient Near East.* Louisville, KY: Westminster John Knox, 2014.

Hemphill, Kenneth S. *The Names of God.* Nashville, TN: B&H Books, 2001.

Hibbs, Pierce Taylor. *The Speaking Trinity and His Worded World: Why Language Is at the Center of Everything.* Eugene, OR: Wipf & Stock, 2018.

Keener, Craig S. *Paul, Women, and Wives: Marriage and Women's Ministry in the Letters of Paul.* Grand Rapids, MI: Baker Academic, 1992.

Kennedy, Jeff S. *A Prophet Mighty in Deed and Word: Jesus' Subversive Reading of the Isaian Jubilee in Luke 4:16–30.* Eugene, OR: Pickwick Publications, 2022.

Köstenberger, Andreas J., and Thomas R. Schreiner, eds. *Women in the Church: An Interpretation and Application of 1 Timothy 2:9–15.* 3rd ed. Wheaton, IL: Crossway, 2016.

Liddell, Henry George, Robert Scott, and Henry Stuart Jones. *A Greek–English Lexicon.* 9th ed. Oxford: Clarendon Press, 1940.

Longfellow, Brenda. "Female Patrons and Honorific Statues in Pompeii." *Memoirs of the American Academy in Rome* 59/60 (2014/2015): 81–101.

Lucian of Samosata. "The Parasite." §49. In *Lucian*, vol. 3, translated by A. M. Harmon. Loeb Classical Library 130. Cambridge, MA: Harvard University Press, 1921.

Mark, Joshua J. "Enuma Elish—The Babylonian Epic of Creation—Full Text." *World History*

Encyclopedia, May 4, 2018. Accessed October 2, 2025.

McDowell, Sean, and Scott Rae. "Truth and Toxic Masculinity." *Think Biblically* (podcast), Biola University, August 3, 2023. Accessed October 2, 2025.

Monte, Lindsay M. "The Two Extremes of Fatherhood." *America Counts*. U.S. Census Bureau, November 5, 2019. Accessed October 2, 2025.

Obladen, M. "From Right to Sin: Laws on Infanticide in Antiquity." *Neonatology* 109, no. 4 (2016): 252–61.

Pearcey, Nancy R. *The Toxic War on Masculinity: How Christianity Reconciles the Sexes*. Ada, MI: Baker, 2023.

Philo of Alexandria. *On the Life of Moses*. Translated by F. H. Colson. In *Philo*, vol. 6, *On Abraham. On Joseph. On Moses*. Loeb Classical Library 289. Cambridge, MA: Harvard University Press, 1935.

Pierce, Ronald W., Cynthia Long Westfall, and Christa L. McKirland, eds. *Discovering Biblical Equality: Biblical, Theological, Cultural, and Practical*

Perspectives. 3rd ed. Downers Grove, IL: IVP Academic, 2021.

Piper, John, and Wayne Grudem, eds. *Recovering Biblical Manhood and Womanhood: A Response to Evangelical Feminism*. Wheaton, IL: Crossway, 1991.

Plutarch. "On Listening to Lectures (De audiendo), 4.1." In *Moralia*, vol. 1, translated by F. C. Babbitt. Loeb Classical Library 197. Cambridge, MA: Harvard University Press, 1927.

Sax, Leonard. *Boys Adrift: The Five Factors Driving the Growing Epidemic of Unmotivated Boys and Underachieving Young Men*. New York: Basic Books, 2007.

Slanski, Kathryn E. "The Law of Hammurabi and Its Audience." *Yale Journal of Law & the Humanities* 24, no. 1 (2012): 97–110.

Skehan, Patrick W., and Alexander A. Di Lella. *The Wisdom of Ben Sira*. Anchor Bible 39. Garden City, NY: Doubleday, 1987.

Smith, Mark S. *The Early History of God: Yahweh and the Other Deities in Ancient Israel*. 2nd ed. Grand Rapids: Eerdmans, 2002.

Stuart, D. "Names, Proper." In *The International Standard Bible Encyclopedia*, rev. ed., edited by Geoffrey W. Bromiley, 3:485–488. Grand Rapids: Eerdmans, 1982.

Wakeman, Mary K. "The Biblical Earth Monster in the Cosmogonic Combat Myth," 313–320 in *Journal of Biblical Literature* 88:3 (Sept 1969).

Wallace-Hadrill, Andrew. "Patronage in Roman Society: From Republic to Empire." In *Patronage in Ancient Society*, edited by Andrew Wallace-Hadrill, 63–87. Leicester-Nottingham Studies in Ancient Society 1. London: Routledge, 1989.

Walton, John H. *Genesis 1 as Ancient Cosmology*. Winona Lake, IN: Eisenbrauns, 2011.

Witthoff, David, ed. *The Lexham Cultural Ontology Glossary*. Bellingham, WA: Lexham Press, 2014.

Zhuang, Sophia. "Men and Women Are Physiologically Unequal: An Equal Research Emphasis." *Yale Scientific Magazine* 93, no. 3 (November 28, 2020). Accessed October 2, 2025.

~~